EVERYDAY
JEWS

To the Jews who serve in the engine room of Jewish life.

To my mother who helped me appreciate their work.

To Deborah, who helped me understand
what it is to be a Jewish leader.

And to my children, who helped me see the absurdities.

EVERYDAY JEWS

Why The Jewish People Are Not
Who You Think They Are

Keith Kahn-Harris

ICON

Published in the UK and USA in 2025 by
Icon Books Ltd, Omnibus Business Centre,
39–41 North Road, London N7 9DP

email: info@iconbooks.com

www.iconbooks.com

ISBN: 978-183773-211-1
ebook: 978-183773-212-8

Typeset by SJmagic DESIGN SERVICES, India

Printed and bound in Great Britain

Contents

About the author

Dr Keith Kahn-Harris is a sociologist and author, based in London. He is a Senior Research Fellow at the Institute for Jewish Policy Research and a Senior Lecturer at Leo Baeck College. He also makes time for pursuing other interests outside the community, including extreme metal music and the warning messages in Kinder Surprise Eggs.

The author of nine books, his most recent publications are *Strange Hate: Antisemitism, Racism and the Limits of Diversity*, *The Babel Message: A Love Letter to Language* (Icon) and (co-authored with Rob Stothard) *What Does A Jew Look Like?* Find out more at kahn-harris.org.

A note on language

I want this book to be read by both Jews and non-Jews. I aim to reveal aspects of Jewish life that Jews rarely think much about and that non-Jews may not know even exist. The challenge I have faced is how to discuss Jewish life without including so much background information that the book starts to look like a textbook that will state the obvious to Jews and appear overly pedagogic to non-Jews.

I have approached this dilemma pragmatically. I do explain some aspects of Jewish life and terminology – hopefully in a concise and efficient way – but not every time. Some elementary aspects of Jewish knowledge are left unexplained or untranslated. We are, after all, living in an online world where the first paragraph of a Wikipedia page will tell you what a common term like 'Shabbat' means.

I have previously written two glossaries that might prove useful to readers. My 2012 book *Judaism: All That Matters* is a short introductory text that explains what Judaism is in a light-hearted way; *What Does a Jew Look Like?*, my 2022 collaboration with the photographer Rob Stothard, portrays a diverse selection of British Jews and includes explanations for key terms. In 2018 I also wrote a factsheet on British Jewry and its multiple denominations and factions for the Religion Media Centre; most of it still holds up and you can find the link in this footnote.[1]

While this book makes an argument about the Jewish people today as a whole, in practice much of the book has a more immediate relevance to particular Jewish communities. My involvement in British Jewish communal life means that many of the examples in the book lean towards the United Kingdom. As the two largest Jewish populations in the world, the American and Israeli Jewish populations are discussed too and, to a lesser extent, I consider European examples as well.

A major challenge I have faced in this, and all the other Jewish books I have written, concerns language. Some of the terms we use in English to describe and classify Jews and Jewish stuff are barely fit for purpose. Classifying Jews as a 'religion' or a 'faith' is too narrow, since not all Jews identify with or practise anything that can be called a religious faith. 'Ethnicity' or (worse) 'race' does not capture the religious side. While 'ethno-religion' is more satisfactory, it's forbiddingly academic, although I have used it occasionally in this book.

At times in this book, I have wanted to find some way of referring to the totality of Jewish being and doing. 'Judaism' is too narrow, so I have used terms like 'Jewishness' or 'Jewish life', which are rather vague. To refer to the collective mass of Jews I veer between 'Jewish people' and 'Jewish community'. I lean towards referring to us as a people when thinking globally and to us as a community when thinking about Jews in a particular location, such as the UK.

Jews differ from each other in ways even more fundamental than geography. One of the main cleavages within the Jewish people is between *Haredi* Judaism and other ways of being and doing Jewish. Haredi Jews (the term translates to 'trembling', or more loosely 'fearful', as in fear of God) are the most 'visible' Jews, the men often wearing black hats, black coats and beards, the women dressed modestly with hair covered. They hold to the strictest interpretations of Jewish law and practice. The term 'Hasidic' is often used to describe them, but it is unsatisfactory, as Hasidic Jews are only one type of Haredi Jew. Indeed, Haredi Judaism is itself highly diverse, with multiple sects and streams. Broadly speaking, what they have in common is a desire to minimise contact with the secular world, ensure that as many men as possible spend as much of their lives as possible in Torah study, and rebuild their numbers after the Holocaust by having extremely large families.

Much of this book discusses and addresses Jews who are not Haredi; who participate in the contemporary world and do not seek isolation from it. However, Haredi Jews are not the only ones whose religious practice is based on a view of Jewish law as divinely ordained. What are sometimes called 'modern orthodox' Jews combine strict adherence to Jewish law with involvement in the non-Jewish world. Under this broad heading, there are also multiple streams. When I refer to 'orthodox' Judaism in this book without further qualification, I am referring to the broad spectrum of practice from Haredi to the progressive end of modern orthodoxy.

My own Jewish practice is, broadly speaking, aligned with 'Reform' Judaism inasmuch as I am a member of a Reform synagogue. There are confusing terminological issues here too. In some countries, this kind of denomination is termed 'Liberal'. In the UK, Reform and Liberal Judaism were two distinct movements, but in 2023 they announced their intention to merge. The new name for the merged movement is likely to be 'Progressive' Judaism, and this is also used as an umbrella term covering the various movements that see Jewish law as 'divinely inspired' but not immutable. Sometimes that includes 'Masorti', or 'Conservative' Judaism – whose practice leans closer to orthodox Judaism – and sometimes it doesn't. When I use 'progressive' in this book I mean non-orthodox Judaisms. When I use 'Reform' in the book, I also mean Liberal Judaism.

'Non-Jews' is an awful term. It defines most of humanity as an absence of Jewishness, which is rather overblown. I have resorted to using it for wont of a better alternative. I've always hated 'gentile' for reasons I can't quite articulate (maybe it sounds forbiddingly Christian?). The Hebrew term 'goy' originally meant something like 'nation' but evolved into meaning non-Jewish people. Today, while not a pejorative term in theory, it can sometimes be used that way, so I have avoided it here.

When it comes to writing about Jewish concepts and practices in English, the whole situation is a mess. Hebrew (and sometimes other languages like Yiddish, Ladino and Aramaic) is woven into the fabric of how Jews name what they believe and what they do. The problem is that there is no single universally agreed standard for transliterating Hebrew into English and other languages. Chanukah is Hanukah is Hanoucca is Hanoukka (the latter two found more commonly in French). While I've tried to go with the most common usages, that's not the end of the problems. It can look clumsy to pluralise a Hebrew word with an English 's', so I've sometimes gone with Hebrew pluralisations, which involve the suffixes -im and -ot (masculine and feminine). Watch out for those. When quoting texts directly, I have been faithful to the transliteration style they use.

A related problem is when to use the Hebrew term and when to use an English one. There is a weird practice in some books of using non-Hebrew terms even when the Hebrew term might be better known. The best example is when *tefillin* are described as 'phylacteries'. You can look both words up if you like. Suffice it to say that I have yet to meet an English speaker who knows what phylacteries are but not what tefillin are.

Consistency is an overrated value. Writing about Jews is a messy business, at least when you do it in English. As this is a book about how Jews and Jewish life are sometimes misrepresented and misunderstood, it makes a curious sort of sense to avoid the pretence that the Jewish people can be summed up in a neat package, tied up with a pretty bow.

Introduction

'What did you do during in the war, Daddy?'

During the war that began on 7 October 2023, I spent much of the time doing what I usually do, communing with my fellow Jews. In that dark period, as I watched Israelis being killed, tortured and kidnapped, shortly followed by Palestinians dying in their thousands, I continued to live my Jewish life. Here are some of things I did in the days following 7 October:

- I attended staff meetings
- I organised travel and accommodation arrangements for a seminar in Brussels
- I confirmed the tech requirements for a hybrid lecture
- I managed to finally sort out my new pension arrangements.

I'm a professional Jew, working for two British Jewish organisations. I believe in the missions of those organisations; one of which trains rabbis and the other which conducts research on Jewish topics. I hold senior positions and do valuable work. But like all jobs, a big part of what I do is pushing paper and coordinating my work with others.

Amid the horrors of the Gaza war, the mundane routines of professional life were a comfort; they provided a spine to my life at a time when everything seemed in flux. That was true for other Jewish professionals whom I know. It was also true for the myriad volunteers on which Jewish organisations rely. Board meetings took place, fundraising dinners happened, synagogues held services. We may have been worrying about Israel–Palestine and fearful of rising antisemitism, but we kept going with everyday Jewish life.

You'd know very little of this if you were to look at press coverage and social media from the period. What you would see is Jews holding vigils and demonstrations, Jews suffering antisemitic attacks, Jews lobbying governments, Jews supporting and condemning the Israeli military, Jews arguing, Jews emoting and Jews feeling.

Of course, this sort of stuff is news; it makes great copy for newspapers and great content for social media. I wouldn't expect to see the headline 'Bar Mitzvah Goes Ahead as Planned'. What was less understandable was how some Jewish newspapers almost completely abandoned coverage of anything other than Israel and antisemitism. In fact, a couple of weeks after the war began, a British rabbi was convicted of downloading child pornography, and it didn't even make the UK Jewish press for several weeks. If that sort of stuff was ignored, what chance was there for more prosaic stories?

This is a common pattern. This book will argue that the image people have of Jews, as well as the image that Jews have of themselves, is profoundly distorted. For a very long time, certainly for the entirety of Christian history, Jews have been seen in much of the world as *important*. That importance means that we are, inevitably, *interesting*. While sometimes this interest can take the form of philosemitic admiration, historically it has more usually provided the foundation of antisemitism. As David Nirenberg argued in his classic history *Anti-Judaism*, the obsessive interest in Jews has been an obsession with understanding and explaining other phenomena *through* the Jews.[1]

The 'Jewish question' (or, more darkly, the 'Jewish problem') emerged in modern Europe following the start of the process of emancipation of Jews that began towards the end of the eighteenth century. As Jews became citizens and left the ghetto, the question arose of what place they could take in this brave new world. The answers to this question divided Jews from themselves and Jews from non-Jews. The Jewish question becoming a kind of tool to think about much bigger questions. That was the case in France at the turn of the twentieth century, when the nation was divided over the fate of Alfred Dreyfus, a Jewish army officer who was falsely accused, unfairly convicted and finally, in 1906, exonerated of treason. When French citizens, the intelligentsia in particular, were discussing whether one French-Jewish man had spied for Germany, they were arguing about the nature of French identity, modern society and whether a religious minority could ever integrate within the French nation.

Today, controversies regarding Israel, the Holocaust and antisemitism have become ways of addressing much bigger sets of questions. The arguments triggered around the world by the Gaza war were also arguments about other things. In the UK, the war has catalysed debates about the future of the Labour Party and the BBC. In the US, the war has been fought over the nature of the modern university. Israelis and Palestinians, Jews and Muslims, have sometimes been reduced to bit-part players in a story that is supposed to be about them.

Non-Jewish fascination in us – philosemitic, antisemitic or any other kind – has inflated the extent to which understanding the Jews means understanding the world. As the bloody history of Israeli–Palestinian conflict shows, huge global interest does not necessarily solve problems.

Jews have colluded in this process. It's hard to see how we could have avoided doing so. When the press comes calling, we have no hesitation in talking about our fears and hopes to a non-Jewish audience. We are outspoken and do not take things lying down. We are very, very interested in ourselves. That doesn't mean that Jews necessarily see themselves as superior. The sense of significance I am talking about is more solipsistic than chauvinistic. While that solipsism is a function of the freedom we now possess, we are still profoundly damaged by the persistent tendency of ourselves and our friends to render us as a question, a puzzle, a conundrum to be solved.

The problem with how important we have become is that we lose the right to simply exist and go about our everyday business. Our public existence risks becoming our whole existence. Jewish life risks being hollowed out as we lose touch with its mundane basis in the fabric of Jewish life. Non-Jews develop a bizarre picture of who we are – and we do too.

In this book I will explore how we misrepresent ourselves and are misrepresented by others; I will also show how Jews can walk themselves back from this questionable existence. I will suggest that the goal of emancipation should never have been the Nobel Prizes we won, the literature we produced, the dazzling brilliance of our involvement in modern societies, states and cultures. Rather, we should have set ourselves the task of becoming an unremarkable sub-group of humanity. We need to look again at the oft-derided possibilities of a parochial form of Jewish community, an inward-looking identity, a modesty about our place in the world.

Of course, the persistence of antisemitism and endless war in Israel–Palestine are not completely under our control. Our enemies and their fantasies about Jews are part of the reason we are so damned interesting. Our 'friends' too will need a lot of persuasion that we are capable of being dull.

What Jews can control is what we value about Jewish existence and how we present what we value to others and to ourselves. Fortunately, there is something valuable in Jewish life that is hidden in plain sight and can provide a different way of understanding who Jews are. It is *everyday* Jewish life that I seek to raise in status. Everyday life is a matter of *doing;* a mass of routines, of mundane, taken-for-granted activities and practices. It's everything from the intricate Jewish laws that govern how orthodox Jews slaughter animals, to the quirks of how secular Jews celebrate Christmas. What I will call *the Jewish way of doing* is distinctive, but it is not extraordinary.

Everyday Jewish doing can even be boring; that is part of its value. When Jews are boring, they unknowingly rebel against the incessant pressure Jews receive to be significant in the world. Boring things keep the world going; they also lay the groundwork for ostensibly 'interesting' things to happen. By valorising the boring, I am valorising the *means* of Jewish life over its ends; the process and the journey rather than the destination.

The everyday is messy and imperfect. That is how most of us live most of the time, in a constant stream of improvisation without undue introspection. The everyday is not precise and exactly defined. This fuzziness is exemplified by my use of the term in the title of this book. I originally wanted to call it 'Boring Jews', but my publisher rightly thought this would lead to misunderstanding. I tried 'Ordinary Jews', but it turns out there's been multiple books published before under this title. I experimented with 'mundane' and 'banal', but these seemed a little highfalutin. So everyday it is; a necessary compromise in a world where the perfect is the enemy of the good.

I openly acknowledge the irony of writing a book for the general public that attempts, through every writerly trick I know, to beguile the reader into accepting that Jews can be dull. There is a precedent for the ironic veneration of dullness. One of the most wonderful and joyous occasions I have participated in was the Boring Conference, which was held annually in London for a few years pre-pandemic. James Ward, the guy that organised the event, is the author of an excellent book on stationery.[2] The conference featured speakers on everything from elevators to roundabouts. I spoke in 2017 about the multilingual warning messages on Kinder Surprise Eggs, an obsession that ultimately turned into a book.[3] The conceit of the event was that apparently boring things can be interesting. That doesn't mean that everyone came away sharing the fascinations of the obsessives who presented. The joy came from witnessing their obsession. So it's possible to find something boring and compelling at the same time. What ties those twin reactions together is a fascination with people. In contrast, while Jews are people and people are fascinated with Jews, that fascination is often based on projection and the erasure of their everyday existence and all too often turns us into symbols of something else.

Even if this book fails to be interesting, even if you don't find Jews interestingly boring, I will still make arguments that are worth giving a hearing to. While Jews may be a pretty extreme case study of the dangers of being significant, the denigration of the everyday and the celebration of the extraordinary is a much bigger phenomenon. In a conflict-ridden world, there is a common insecurity that drives us to justify our existence. A nation, or an aspirant nation, must have an extraordinary culture. An ethnic group must be colourful. An individual must be articulate. Just getting on with the stuff of life is rarely 'enough'. And God help you if you are a trainspotter, literally or figuratively, and revel in the little details that make up the whole …

This book, then, makes the case to my fellow Jews that we should not hide our everyday capacity for dullness, and makes the case to non-Jews that they should let us 'come out' as uninteresting. Perhaps this process can console Jews during a time of unbearable significance. My approach won't stop antisemitism, at least not in the short term. It won't help heal our irreconcilable differences over Israel. But it might help us survive the turmoil. It will definitely help in cooling the ardour of our supposed allies who are so enthralled by our importance. Maybe in the long term we might become too dull to hate, to love or even to bother to know in the first place.

This is a counter-intuitive approach to Jewish survival. I was brought up, like many other Jews, on stories of heroic Jewish activists, such as Emma Goldman or Rabbi Joshua Heschel. I was taught that we are on this earth to 'repair the world' (*tikkun olam*). This is the version of the 'chosen people' that progressive Jews of my era embraced. Obviously, I am not arguing against Jewish activism and doing good in the world. I am suggesting, though, that Jews like me may need to consider the unimaginable – that quietist parochialism, keeping your head down and concentrating on doing everyday Jewish stuff may have a value that we dismissed prematurely. If we aren't to be swallowed up by our lofty values, we have to recover a sense of the lowly value of just getting through the day.

This book asks – pleads even – non-Jewish readers to let us be boring. I hope that non-Jews who read this book will be persuaded to not just let Jews be uninteresting, but also to revel in their own everyday mundanity. And God knows, in an age of anxiety, of endemic war, pandemics, fury and division, we need to be grounded in something other than existential angst. Too often we respond to a fractious world by latching onto the 'big issues', fighting fundamental fights about values and ideologies. In doing so we can lose sight of the multitudinous activity that actually makes us human and makes us social. This is the domain of the minutiae that define the uniqueness of individual lives, cultures and civilisations. It's a domain that can be experienced as boring even when it is quirky and strange when held up to the light. That is its magic.

As a sociologist, I have been thinking and writing about mundane everydayness and how it intersects with the extraordinary for many years, particularly in my work on metal music and culture.[4] However, as a Jew, it is only relatively recently that I have come to embrace the everyday as a Jewish ideal. Doing so has led me to question many of the assumptions I had regarding what Jews should be. I can't quite believe I have come to this point. It's been a surprising journey, and it didn't start on 7 October 2023 but earlier that year, on a Polish baseball field …

Chapter One
Baseball in the bloodlands

A question of survival
How am I going to survive this?

That was the question I asked myself as I boarded the coach at Warsaw Airport. I'd been in a foul mood since my flight landed and I was in a foul mood as I got off the coach at Warsaw Airport a week later. In fact, I was in a foul mood for much of the time I toured the land of my Polish ancestors.

I didn't expect that I would feel so *angry*. This was, after all, my chance to get a taste of the good stuff, that addictive morbidity of which Jewish writers' careers are made. Here I would – finally! – become part of the story. I would walk the streets where my family, the Rojers of Kutno, once lived. I would mourn the ghost of their presence in the traces that remain of Jewish Poland. I would visit the extermination camp where they were murdered. And I would grieve.

But it all felt wrong from the start.

The first warning sign was the convenience store in Warsaw Airport. I'd popped in to buy a sandwich and was distracted by the other Polish products on sale. There was Polish kombucha! When I visit a country I adore exploring convenience store products, particularly strange and wonderful soft drinks. I realised that I was going to enjoy this trip … Until

I remembered what I was actually here for. I bought a cheese sandwich and trudged off to find my group at the designated meeting point.

I sat alone on a double seat on the bus, surrounded by excited and nervous Jews (mostly older than me) getting to know each other. I plugged in my earphones. Tonight was the night of the Eurovision Song Contest, the first time I would be separated from my family for the event since my wife and I had children. I tried to join in by listening to the show on streaming radio and texting my kids on WhatsApp. It wasn't the same. And when I tried to tell a new acquaintance that I was missing Eurovision, she was only interested in how the Israeli entrant would do.

The memorial tour was organised by a group of Jewish descendants of central Poland. Our group included Jews from the UK, USA, Canada, Australia and Israel. Most people were lovely and the organisers had put together a packed itinerary, with the help of local Poles who were keen to commemorate the vanished Jewish presence in their towns.

The people weren't what annoyed me about the tour. And I couldn't fault the programme. So what was it that was triggering me? On the trip from the airport I gazed out the window at the Polish branch of IKEA, at road signs, gas stations and adverts, and tried to work out what I was feeling. As the tour progressed, I felt myself yearning for something I couldn't quite name. I kept being intrigued by shops, the countryside, the forests and rivers, together with the urban fabric of the towns we visited. I kept having to remind myself what I was here to do. On the day we visited Kutno, I tried to focus as we toured what remained of Jewish life – the cemetery the Nazis destroyed, the dilapidated ruins of the ghetto.

Halfway through the week, I took a day off and hired a car. On that beautiful spring day, my heart soared as I drove parallel to the wide Vistula through sun-dappled woods, and onward to the picturesque town of Płock (the hometown of a different branch of my family). I walked around the Jewish district, bought a Polish kombucha and a Polish Kinder Surprise Egg. Then I drove on to Kutno, this time alone.

As I drove into the grounds of the campus on the outskirts of the town, I realised that this was it. This was what I was really here for, even if I couldn't admit it to anyone else in the group (or to my mother, who had desperately wanted to join the tour but was unable to due to my father's advancing dementia).

I was here to find out about Polish baseball.

The diamond gleamed in the spring sunshine, awaiting the new season with intense anticipation. The grass was perfectly cropped, the pitcher's mound neat and tidy, the bases had not a single scuff mark. The stands, soon to be filled with cheering supporters, were silent. There were *five* diamonds at the Europejskie Centrum Małej Ligii Basebolowej. Two of them were adult-sized, used by the local club Stal Kutno. The rest were smaller, designed to host the European Little League baseball championships every July.

I was given a tour of the complex by Waldemar Szymański, the man who was instrumental in bringing to the town a facility that any American city would be proud of. I wanted to know how baseball came to Kutno, but he also wanted to know how *I* came to Kutno.

In 2013, I was invited to give a talk at a TEDx event in Krakow. My topic was 'small worlds', how little communities are spaces of quiet heroism and meaning. I suggested to the audience that if you were to choose a small world at random, you'd inevitably find interesting stories. I challenged them to find something out about a small world I assumed existed but knew absolutely nothing about – the baseball scene in Poland.

A few weeks later a journalist who had attended my talk got in touch to tell me that Polish baseball was a bigger deal than I'd thought. In fact, he'd written an entire article on the subject, focusing on the European Little League Baseball Centre in Kutno. My interest in small worlds collided with my family history. When I arrived at the baseball centre I suddenly got what it was that I was yearning for, the absence of which was making me furious with frustration.

It was *life* that was missing. Life in all its mundanity and strange beauty; life as ordinary, routine, yet somehow extraordinary; the sort of life that we only notice when it is absent. I found that life in the form of Waldemar Szymański. An old man with health problems, his passion for what he had built shone through nevertheless. He almost cried with pride as he showed me his legacy.

Baseball has been played in Poland as early as the 1950s. It was brought to Kutno in 1984 by a Cuban, Juan Echevarria Motola, who had married a local woman he'd met when they were at university together in Prague. In the late 1980s, Waldemar fell in love with the game at a demonstration event; too old to play himself, he started umpiring, encouraged his son to take up the sport, and soon became a significant figure in the national baseball association. Aided by the support of the Polish-American Major League player Stan Musial, Waldemar managed to attract the European Little League Centre to the town in the mid-1990s.

Baseball has been good to Waldemar. He travelled the world, attended matches all over the US and became a member of the Polish Olympic Committee. And the world came to Kutno, to his town.

I wasn't supposed to be here for the living, for baseball stadiums and nice old Polish men. I was supposed to be a temporary sojourner in a Poland that was long gone, where millions of Jews once lived and sometimes thrived. A place from which Jews were ripped with extreme violence; hundreds of years of life destroyed in just six. And while it was not Poles who perpetrated the genocide that wiped out the Polish branches of my family, that didn't mean Poland was a place of innocence. The lengthy history of Polish antisemitism, particularly the post-war campaigns that saw most of the Jews who had survived the Holocaust leave the country, makes many Jews uneasy with Poles. While the local contacts we met seemed to be enthusiastic about commemorating Jewish life, our group debated their sincerity and possible ulterior motives.

Although some of the Americans in the group were intrigued by the existence of Polish baseball, most of the time Polish everyday life was only a backdrop to the *real* story, our story, an extraordinary and terrible story, a story that marked us out and made us irreducibly *different*. I don't mind being different. In fact, I love my Jewish difference. But on my trip to Poland I felt an almost physical aversion to *this* kind of difference. While I felt proud and honoured to be the first family member to return to Kutno in order to remember those who had been murdered, I resented my new identity as 'Holocaust-obsessed Jew coming back to the old country'. Sometimes I felt like what has been termed a 'stuffed Jew', a living museum exhibit, visiting a place of lifeless relics.[1]

Being part of the story

As a writer, it would be quite helpful if I *was* that kind of Jew. I am acutely aware that the Holocaust is hot stuff. It is the font of an endless torrent of stories: of murder, of suffering, of resilience and escape. Jews and non-Jews alike are drawn to the life stories of Primo Levi, Elie Wiesel, Anne Frank and to any number of other accounts.

I had always assumed that I could never be part of that story. My grandparents were all the children or grandchildren of those who got out of Poland before the First World War. I was brought up knowing that some of my distant ancestors never made it out and were never heard from again. In retirement, my mother started to fill in the blanks of our family history. In the process she discovered the group who were to organise the memorial tour I participated in.

The more I found out about my ancestors, the more I became aware of what we would never know. When I visited the Polish addresses we had managed to find, at which family members had at some point lived, I felt a certain sense of satisfaction, but it didn't make them come to life. I don't have enough to build a story out of. My Polish family lived and were murdered. That's it. I will never get to write a Holocaust book about my family. On the trip I felt an unsettling mix of anger and disappointment at my own narcissism, as well as at the Holocaust obsessions of Jews and non-Jews alike.

When I returned to London, I published an article that attempted to work through what I had experienced on the Poland trip (self-censoring the anger and thwarted writerly ambition).[2] I talked about the final place we visited, the extermination camp at Chełmno where my ancestors were likely murdered. The disturbing emptiness of the forest clearing in which it was situated, the lack of bodies, the lack of knowledge, seemed to represent a kind of void, a profound *lack* that we desperately seek to fill with stories. In my article I admitted that, while I certainly didn't feel nothing, I was very much aware that I had no one to mourn – just names of ancestors about whose everyday lives we know nothing. I shared the article with the group and, while most of them seemed to appreciate what I was trying to say, one of the organisers of the trip emailed me as follows:

> When I was in 'our towns' I sensed the vibrant and difficult life our ancestors lived. When I was in Chełmno, I felt the terror of a five year old child hanging to his mother's hand who wanted to live but had run out of options.

The extraordinary presumption – to know what a five-year-old about to be gassed might feel – seemed to me to be a way of filling the nothingness with something. More darkly, it's also an example of how sorrow can become a kind of currency, a claim to some kind of status as mourner.

Refusing to be a dead Jew

There are incentives for Jews and non-Jews to focus on the negative aspects of Jewish experience. I see this in my professional life all the time. One of my jobs is to run the European Jewish Research Archive, an online repository of social research on European Jewish populations.[3] Over the years, the proportion of research publications devoted to contemporary antisemitism, or to Holocaust memorialisation, has risen inexorably; in 2022 such publications constituted half of the total.[4] There are few incentives to research European Jewish *life*. Funding is much more accessible for those who wish to research dead Jews and threatened Jews.

Look, I love to settle down with a good book about the Holocaust as much as the next person. Holocaust stories are endlessly alluring, not despite their horror, but because of it. They are stories about life pushed to the limit and beyond, about the very boundaries of what human beings are capable of inflicting and enduring.

I have always refused to place the genocide of my people at the heart of my Jewish identity. Of course, I do still have some sympathy with the argument that choosing to identify as Jewish is a retrospective slap in the face to the Jew-haters, Nazis most of all. This is what the rabbi and philosopher Emil Fackenheim called the '614th commandment' (there are 613 in the Torah), to 'not hand Hitler a posthumous victory'.[5] Stubborn defiance aside, there are so many good things about Jewish life, in all its diversity, that placing the Holocaust at the centre of Jewish identity seems tantamount to treating the good stuff as unimportant. The same goes for antisemitism. While Jews need to understand and fight anti-semitism, we should be doing so in order to make it easier, safer and less stressful to live distinctive Jewish lives. Those of us who write about contemporary antisemitism should be doing so with the aspiration that, in the future, antisemitism will only be of interest to historians.

The problem is that some Jews and non-Jews are so fixated on antisemitism and the Holocaust that they come across as uninterested in Jewish life. That's understandable – although by no means always the case – for those who directly experienced the Holocaust, or whose parents, grandparents or other close relations did. What's the excuse of non-Jews who take on Holocaust remembrance or fighting antisemitism as their cause, yet are apathetic or ignorant of other aspects of Jewish existence?

It's all too easy to treat Jews as if they are Charlie Brown, living under a permanent grey cloud. Jews do it too. The US writer Dara Horn's 2021 book *People Love Dead Jews* skewered the ways in which a fascination with Jewish suffering is often combined with limited respect or understanding for actually existing Jews.[6] The trouble is that Horn herself doesn't seem to escape the trap. Her book is serious, angry and (with the exception of the final chapter in which she extols study of the Talmud) treats Jews as labouring under the weight of unbearable grief and fear. But not everyone is as crushingly serious as Horn is. Sometimes Jewishness is worn lightly. It's as though she cannot see the texture of Jewish life that is hiding in plain sight. Ironically, Horn's book is popular because she ultimately feeds into the demand for Jews to be weighty and angsty. People love dead Jews because we let them.

The anger I experienced in Poland was the culmination of years of frustration. During the period when Jeremy Corbyn led the British Labour Party, I was in demand as a writer who could help people understand the antisemitism controversy that swirled around him. I wrote many articles for the *Guardian* and other newspapers; I wrote a book, *Strange Hate: Antisemitism, Racism and the Limits of Diversity*, that analysed why antisemitism in the left is so controversial; I spoke to Jewish and non-Jewish audiences about what was going on. All this was good for my career, but in the end I became infuriated by the precipitous gap between the interest shown in antisemitism and the apathy towards other aspects of Jewish existence. Sadly, Jews were as responsible for that gap as non-Jews.

By the time I got to Poland I had had just about enough of negative Jewish identities. I resented being forced to inhabit a Jewish identity that was removed from everyday existence. It was only in my visit to the baseball centre that I felt that I was *here*, *now*. For most of the trip I felt I had been forced into inhabiting a negative Jewish space that was completely removed from our actual surroundings. That's often how Jews have lived, separated by force from the rest of society. But I'm a Jew from a place and time where it is possible to see no contradiction between living Jewishly in all its fullness and living where I happened to be. It's true that it's easier for me than others. I grew up in the UK at a time when antisemitism was at a tolerable level. I am not a visibly orthodox Jew so I can easily 'pass' wherever I want. I am Jewish everywhere, and also other things too. In Poland I got a glimpse of a Jewishness removed from its environment and I did not like it. While this has helped me empathise with generations of Jews who were similarly set apart in antisemitic societies, this time we had set ourselves apart voluntarily.

In Jewish tradition, we are supposed to be separate from others, at least to some degree. The closest translation of 'holy' in Hebrew is *kodesh*, but its sense is very different; it implies being set apart, removed, dedicated to the divine. The 'chosenness' of the chosen people implies not so much selected to be privileged, exulted and better than anyone else, more that we are chosen to receive the yoke of rigorous responsibility to keep the arduous instructions of the divine. What can sound like Jewish supremacy is, in fact, a burden. While this burden is not necessarily of the Charlie Brown variety, it's easy to see how it can become so.

How do we reconcile the desire that Jews have for separateness with our desire not to be hated for it? How do we mourn the suffering of Jews without becoming defined by that suffering? How can a Jew like me go to mourn his ancestors without feeling like they are removed from the world? And how can we get both Jews and non-Jews to show more interest in the manifold other dimensions of Jewishness?

Even asking such questions can reproduce the problem. If we see Jewishness as a problem to be addressed through angst-ridden analysis, we can simply replace one kind of obsessive focus on Jews with another.

There is a way out: To acknowledge that there is a bigger issue at work here. One that impacts on all of us to some degree, Jewish or not …

The extraordinary and the everyday

Like those dinosaurs who could only see their prey when it was in motion, human beings are programmed to look for the extraordinary, for some kind of change against the background foliage. That capacity to focus on that which stands out allows us to 'see' the differences between individual humans and groups of humans. While to see difference doesn't necessarily mean hating that difference, it's a short step from finding the extraordinary alluring to finding the extraordinary disgusting.

The allure of difference also affects how we see ourselves. That which is not in motion, the solid stuff of life, is often taken for granted, invisible. It's rarely what humans take pride in. Rather, as individuals and groups we exult in our extraordinariness.

That's certainly how Jews have found the strength to endure during times of persecution. It's also how Jews defend themselves when under attack. But even for Jews who don't see themselves this way theologically, the rhetoric of extraordinariness is never far away: Some of us write books about how many Nobel Prize winners we have, some of us explain how unique the Holocaust was and contemporary antisemitism is, some of us exult in the 'miracle' of the modern state of Israel, some of us exult in the anti-fascist tradition that opposes Zionism. Left or right, religious or secular, orthodox or reform, Jews identify as extraordinary. Jewish everyday life is too unremarkable to notice, too boring to write about, too mundane to tell us anything.

In my graduate training in sociology, I was introduced to a different way of thinking about everyday life, one that focuses on the taken-for-granted aspects of existence. Rather than seeking out the inner core of human being – through interviews and other intrusive methods – the sociologists I came to admire, such as Harvey Sacks and Howard Garfinkel (both Jews), argued that we should look at the myriad tiny ways through which human social life is reproduced; the endless process of recreating the world anew from moment to moment. Everyday life is humanity's greatest achievement, and the more prosaic it appears, the more important it is.

That sociological tradition taught me that humans are never just 'being' in the world; we accomplish being through *doing*. We aren't bored, we do boredom. We aren't Jews, we do Jewish. All peoples have their own idiosyncratic ways of doing. The Jewish way of doing isn't better than anyone else's. *How* we do everyday life is one of the things that makes us distinctive.

There's a Yiddish phrase I am quite fond of, *mach Shabbes*: 'make the Sabbath', or basically 'get on with it'. The Sabbath is welcomed on Friday by a series of religious rituals that take time to perform. They also precede the Sabbath meal, which is usually an elaborate one. So, to exclaim *mach Shabbes* when someone is faffing around simultaneously means 'get on with the ritual' and 'get on with the meal, I'm starving'. Jews are constantly pushing themselves and others to get on with the next thing. It doesn't matter if the next thing is something sacred; to treat even the most apparently 'serious' aspects of Jewishness as worthy of lingering over is to invite impatience.

Onward, ever onward.

We build things. We organise. We collaborate, network and create community. We have survived, and even flourished, in a huge variety of historical circumstances, in conditions both benign and hostile. When things go well, we create things. When things go badly, we create things. A threat is an opportunity for a new organisation, a new campaign, a new movement. We do things in defiance of hope or experience.

We do things even when we don't believe in what we are doing. We are a people of strictly orthodox atheists, ritual-loving secularists, Diaspora Zionists who go on tours of Israel for the sex, and anti-Zionists who live in Israel just because. The Jewish way of doing resolves all contradiction.

Doing Jewish is often boring, exhausting and relentless. That's what makes a Jewish life a life worth living.

Another question of survival
How are we going to survive this?

It was incredibly self-indulgent of me to ask how I was going to survive a trip to Poland in spring 2023. The catering was excellent, the accommodation pleasant, the people often delightful. I guess it shows how far we've come that the worst a Jew can face in Poland is not having enough time to explore convenience stores.

A few months later, though, Jews had occasion to ask this existential question in far more serious circumstances. The Hamas attacks on 7 October 2023 and the Gaza war that followed have not united Jews or Israelis in terms of values and politics, but it may have united us in asking how we will survive this period. For some, the physical survival of Jews in Israel and the Diaspora has come into question. For others, particularly on the left, it is our moral survival that is in question. It's been a heavy, heavy time.

The question that isn't being asked as much as it should be is how everyday Jewish life can survive this: With Jews so much in the spotlight, facing existential questions, will we ever find Jewish life mundane again?

Throughout this period, I've been feeling something akin to what I felt in Poland, albeit with a bit more justification. It seems like we Jews are being ripped out of the realm of the ordinary, into the realm of the extraordinary. We are colluding in this process; in fact, we may sometimes be leading it in our desire to make our voices heard. And against this backdrop I feel the kind of envy I felt for the everyday citizens of Kutno.

The Eurovision Song Contest once again played a central part in this unwanted drama. During Eurovision 2023 I resented being separated from my family to do 'serious' stuff. I watched Eurovision 2024 at home with my family, but I still felt alienated from a precious touchstone in my calendar. This Eurovision took place in the shadow of massive protests against Israel's participation in the event. Many of the competitors clearly resented the presence of the Israeli entrant, Eden Golan, and boos could be heard during her performance and in the vote counting (as well as some cheers). She came fifth in the end, delighting many Jews of my acquaintance, for whom it was a triumph against the bullying of a twenty-year-old woman and of an entire people by extension.

For me, it didn't really matter how Israel did in the contest. While I have views on boycotts of Israel, they were irrelevant here. What upset me was that, whoever won, the beautiful and ridiculous space of Eurovision had become fraught and tainted *and we were the reason for it*. I resented the boycotters, resented the anti-boycotters, resented everyone who denied me what I needed by making this Eurovision *all about us*.

It's this kind of attention that I wonder whether we can survive. I might be more optimistic if more Jews were pushing back and fighting for the everyday. At the moment, though, we are immersed in the extraordinary. Pushing back means recognising not just where we are now, but how deeply we have misrepresented who we are – to ourselves and to everyone else.

Chapter Two

The secrets of the Jews

Downplaying doing

Sometime at the end of the 2000s, I had a long conversation with an old schoolfriend, a Jewish professional like me. Unlike me, he had emigrated to Israel after university. At the time of our conversation, he had returned to the UK to run a Jewish organisation. He explained that, while he was perfectly comfortable in the UK and liked many aspects of the country, it wasn't a 'serious' part of his identity. It was Israel, the Jewish state, where he felt he really belonged. As he put it, 'I like Marmite, but it's not part of my identity.'

To see something like a fondness for Marmite as unrelated to the 'serious' stuff of identity underestimates the importance of such apparent triviality in making a nation. Doing British things like eating British food products is as important to British national identity as taking pride in the royal family. That is how 'doing nationhood' works.

Perhaps we Jews downplay the Jewish way of doing because we have learned that this is not what non-Jews respect. Jewish vulnerability is such that we often feel we need a big story to secure our place in the world. Perhaps also, Jews in countries with a Christian past or present have internalised a sense that Jews are a 'religion' in the Christian mould. While all forms of Christianity involve doing things (as well as not doing other things), at their heart are belief, faith and salvation – matters of the soul and matters of the next world. The Jewish way of doing is so focused on doing things in this human world that it makes for an odd fit in societies where belief is of such central importance.

Too often, then, Jews fit into the Western world through giving the impression that Jewishness is a matter of being rather than doing. But it is a turbulent kind of being that we perform, an epic existential struggle through which Jews attempt to find a place in this world.

In February 2023, the novelist Howard Jacobson gave a keynote lecture at London's Jewish Book Week.[1] The title was 'How the Jews Invented Disappointment'. What struck me most when I read the lecture in the *Jewish Chronicle* the following week was what he *didn't* mention. Here are a few selected quotes. Can you tell what is missing?

> ... Today I'd say that what defines Jews essentially is disappointment. Disappointment, the non-fulfilment of expectation, is the mournful poetry of the Jewish soul. Not only what we're good at, but what explains – what helps explain, at least – how it is, to the disappointment of others, that we are still here.
>
> ... Who could have blamed the Jews if, disillusioned, abandoned, defeated and ashamed, they had ripped up their prayer books and switched allegiance to more successful deities? Yet this the defeated Jews did not do. Schooled to expect the worst, they made poetry out of it.
>
> ... The fact is, Jews don't do messiahs. We might have conceived them but we want them to remain a concept.
>
> ... We are – to our glory – a people incapable of living in peace with ourselves. But the idealistic, tirelessly self-critical Jew is not the same as the ashamed Jew who believes every malevolent anti-Jewish whisper he hears.

What's missing here and in the lecture as a whole is any reference to Jews doing things. Jacobson's thesis – that Jewish being
is defined by a creative and productive kind of disappointment –
has a lot to recommend it, but this isn't why I have quoted
liberally from it. The 'data' upon which he builds his thesis is
broadly literary; he quotes from the Bible, Franz Kafka, David
Grossman, Harold Bloom, among others. He paints a picture of
a Jewish people engaged in an endless, often tortuous struggle
to understand who Jews are and who Jews must be.

Jacobson is a man of letters, a writer and critic whose world
is on the page and whose life is an endless struggle to articulate
what it is to be (Jewish or otherwise). To a hammer, everything
looks like a nail. The Jewish people is full of such hammers; we
produce an extraordinary number of writers, artists, musicians
and academics who grapple, often very publicly, with what it is
to be Jewish, with antisemitism and its legacies, and the vexed
question of what Jews' place in the world should be. That struggle can lead to scintillating art, to dazzling wit, to profound
rumination. As the British critic Norman Lebrecht puts it, the
Jewish 'genius' in modernity is inseparable from 'anxiety':

> Jews in the nineteenth century and the first half of the twentieth
> are gripped by a dread that their rights to citizenship and free
> speech will be revoked. After the Dreyfus Trial, great minds are
> driven by a need to justify their existence in a hostile environ-
> ment and to do it quickly, before the next pogrom. They do not
> expect acceptance. On the contrary, knowing that their ideas
> are likely to be rejected leaves them free to think the unthink-
> able, and forced to do so at speed, before the next crisis.[2]

In her book *Feeling Jewish*, another British Jew, the academic
Devorah Baum, argues that 'feelings are like Jews, Jews are like

feelings'.³ What she means by this is that Jews have played an important role in revealing and dissecting the difficult feelings that the turbulent course of modernity has sparked. Feelings, like Jews, can be 'unwanted', though. As with Lebrecht, for Baum Jews seem fated to play a revelatory and disruptive role in the modern world.

I don't deny the cultural treasures that Jewish anxiety has produced. The trouble is that the presence of so much striking Jewish culture ends up giving a particular kind of Jew an outsize role in defining who Jews are both to ourselves and to the rest of the world. That kind of Jew is rarely one who does much everyday Jewish stuff, let alone one who does it with other Jews. We rarely hear from the Jews who stolidly keep the show on the road: the synagogue committee members, the Sunday morning *cheder* teachers, the Jews in the pews, the Jews that feel the angst but do it anyway.

Every year, Channel 4 airs an 'alternative Christmas message' on British television as an accompaniment to the monarch's Christmas message aired on the BBC. In 2023 they chose the actor and comedian Stephen Fry. While he has never hidden his Jewishness, he is much better known for embodying a particular kind of traditional English wit. In his Christmas message he both affirmed and undercut his Jewishness:⁴

One truth about myself, however, that I never thought for one single second would ever be an issue about which I had any cause to worry in this country, was that I'm a Jew. Yes, you heard me correctly, I am a Jew. That may surprise some people. It surprises me, really. I don't think of myself as especially Jewish. Indeed, sometimes people rather embarrassingly refer to me as 'quintessentially English', whatever that means … But if you take a swab of my spittle – as I did with one of those genetic services – up comes 52 per cent Ashkenazi Jew. More than half, which was a bit of a surprise. My mother's Jewish family came over from Central Europe in the 1930s, but my father died without knowing that he was a fraction Jewish. Maybe you are a fraction Jewish too without knowing it. Does it matter? I mean, I don't really 'identify as Jewish' any more than I 'identify as English' or British.

The core of Fry's Christmas message was this:

> At this time in the face of the greatest rise in anti-Jewish racism since records began, Jews should stand upright and proud in who they are. And so should you, whatever your genetic makeup.

This was a welcome message for many British Jews to hear at an anxious time. Of course, not all agreed. Another British Jewish comedian, Alexei Sayle, a longtime stalwart of the anti-Zionist left, recorded an 'alternative alternative Christmas message'.[5] Defining himself as an 'elderly Jewish comedian', he opined:

> One of the elderly Jewish comedians has urged us all to stand with the Jewish people. Well, fair enough. The Jews I'm going to stand with are those of the Jewish bloc who I've marched with on all the pro-Palestine demonstrations ... If you want to stand with Jewish people, stand with the Jewish bloc.

Alexei Sayle is the kind of Jew that other Jews sometimes disparage as an 'AsAJew', one who, it is claimed, 'uses' his Jewish identity only to attack Israel and other Jews. Yet Stephen Fry is as uninvolved, as he freely admits, as Sayle is. Both recorded their messages against the backdrop of a Christmas tree.

I am not saying that Jews like Fry and Sayle are 'lesser' Jews. The problem is that Jews who have the most prominent public podiums are often, like Fry and Sayle, those whose Jewishness is largely a matter of being, of values and identifications. It's understandable, therefore, that non-Jews end up underestimating or ignoring Jews who do. Those Jews are, too often, invisible Jews ...

Comic misrepresentations

We don't help ourselves. When Jews represent Jewish life in the public sphere, Jewish doing usually takes second place to Jewish being. That leads to the strange phenomenon of Jews misrepresenting Jewish practice, even when they know better.

Take the series *The Marvelous Mrs. Maisel*, which aired on Amazon Prime between 2017 and 2023. Over five seasons, the show follows Miriam 'Midge' Maisel, a privileged New York Jewish housewife, as she discovers a talent for comedy and struggles to become a successful standup. It is loosely inspired by the career of Joan Rivers, and Lenny Bruce appears as a character in some episodes.

The first episode begins with Midge making a brilliantly witty speech at her lavish wedding reception in 1958.[6] She ends with the throwaway line, 'And yes, there is shrimp in the egg rolls.' Cue pandemonium. Midge's mother desperately follows an outraged man who is walking out in disgust, pleading, 'Rabbi, she's kidding!' And how do we know he is a rabbi? Because he is wearing a *tallit*, a prayer shawl.

The wedding scene is meant to establish Midge's character as someone who, when we first meet her, is embedded in middle-class Jewish life. She has a talent for wit and mischief that often flummoxes her family. And yes, a rabbi from pretty much any Jewish denomination would likely be outraged if there was shrimp in the egg rolls at a wedding; so would many of the guests.

So what's the problem?

Well, no rabbi from any Jewish denomination – and no guest, for that matter – would ever wear a *tallit* to a wedding reception. The *tallit* is worn by the person leading prayers and by the congregation as a whole at morning prayer services. At Jewish wedding ceremonies, the groom (and, in some progressive Jewish denominations, the bride) may wear a *tallit*. At a wedding *reception* nobody wears one. A rabbi at a wedding reception, or a traditionally observant person at a wedding reception, may wear a *tallit katan*, but this is an undergarment rather than a shawl, worn permanently and not always visibly.

Another example: The British sitcom *Friday Night Dinner*, which aired for six seasons between 2011 and 2020, made no bones about its Jewishness. The programme is about the Goodman family, Jews living in a north London suburb. Every Friday night the two twenty-something Goodman sons come home for dinner. Friday night marks the start of *Shabbat*, the Sabbath, and this is widely celebrated with a special family dinner, even in fairly secular Jewish households.

The writer of *Friday Night Dinner*, Robert Popper, grew up in a north London Jewish environment, and some of the regular cast were Jewish. The show was a hit and is much-loved in the north London Jewish community. Jewishness is a major theme in the programme, as one would expect, and a frequent source of its humour. In particular, the Goodmans' oddball neighbour, Jim, is enthralled by their Jewishness even though he has almost no understanding of what it means. When the Goodmans finally invite Jim for dinner (very reluctantly), he turns up wearing what he calls a 'little hat', made out of a torn-out square of his shirt, exclaiming repeatedly and inappropriately, 'Shalom!'

So what's the problem?

While the Goodman household is not very religious, they are traditional enough that gathering for Friday night dinner is an unquestioned rule. On or next to the dinner table, we observe the ritual objects associated with Shabbat: the lit candles, silver wine cups and the platted *chollah* loaf. Yet no one on the show ever even says the word 'Shabbat', or the Yiddish alternative *Shabbes*, let alone 'Shabbat dinner'. We never see the candles being lit or the bread cut, let alone hear the blessings associated with these actions. Even in very non-religious households, it would be surprising if a family that treated Shabbat dinner as an immovable date would never refer to Shabbat or would go to the bother of assembling the ritual items without even a token attempt at the blessings. After all, you can do the bare minimum in less than a minute.

I admit that it is possible that some Jewish households mark the Sabbath as the Goodmans do, but *Friday Night Dinner* also features aspects of Judaism as practised in north London that *never* happen. In one episode, which, in a break from the norm, takes place on a Sunday, the family gather to attend the funeral of the kids' great uncle, the brother of the appallingly brilliant character 'horrible grandma'.[7] The boys are informed that they will be carrying the coffin. They aren't happy about this, as their great uncle was hugely obese and they hardly knew him anyway. At the funeral itself, the boys and the other pallbearers struggle to carry the coffin to the grave; they end up dropping it, smashing it in the process. Jim's dog, Wilson, who is ravenous, ends up chowing down on the uncle.

It's a hilarious episode but a wilfully inaccurate one. Pallbearers feature in Jewish funerals conducted in some Jewish communities, including Sweden and parts of the US. But British north London Jewish funerals *never* feature pall-bearers, at least if they are conducted in a Jewish cemetery (as is the case here). It's ironic that we are invited to laugh at Jim's inappropriate behaviour at the funeral – turning up, uninvited, with his dog, carrying black helium balloons – when the funeral itself would be seen as inappropriate if any north London Jewish family attempted to conduct it in the way the Goodmans do.

In both *Friday Night Dinner* and *The Marvelous Mrs. Maisel*, the Jews involved in the production knew that they were including Jewishly implausible scenes *and they did it anyway*. The reason I am confident about making that claim is because none of these examples require much Jewish knowledge to deconstruct, you just need to have spent a bit of time in a Jewish community. We also know that they know better because, in other respects, both series are infused with accurate depictions of Jewish life. In *The Marvelous Mrs. Maisel* we visit a Jewish resort in the Catskills and get to know the claustrophobic world of Upper West Side Jewish dating. In *Friday Night Dinner*, having myself grown up in the milieu it depicts, I can attest to the subtle and not-so-subtle ways in which it recalls the words, gestures, speech rhythms and behaviours that are so familiar to me.

Despite the note-perfect accuracy of some scenes, in this kind of Jewish cultural production it is only an optional extra. What comes first is fidelity to something less tangible: the nebulously angsty, awkward kind of Jewishness that is so attractive to culture creators. From this standpoint, it makes sense for the funeral in *Friday Night Dinner* to feature pallbearers, as the ultimately disastrous consequences reveal the klutziness of young Jewish men. A rabbi wearing a *tallit* at a wedding reception makes sense, as it accentuates how many Jews see rabbis as upholders of standards.

There are whole swathes of doing that have rarely been put on film, such as the thousands of Jewish charities with their thousands of trustees and board members. Sitting on committees is a big part of Jewish doing and potentially a rich source of comedy. Jackie Goodman, the matriarch on *Friday Night Dinner*, would almost certainly have sat on multiple committees. Yet we see almost nothing of her Jewish life other than her family and friends.

One might argue that Jews in the creative industries are disproportionately more likely to be secular Jews and they may be somewhat insecure about getting Jewish religious practice wrong, or they may simply not know what they don't know. Yet even 'secular' Jews are often deeply engaged in doing, including apparently 'religious' things. In any case, even creative works that engage with more overtly religious forms of Judaism sometimes soft-peddle the enormous number of things that religious Jews must do. The Israeli TV drama *Shtisel*, which found a global audience via Netflix, depicts the lives of a strictly orthodox family in Jerusalem, but we rarely see them praying, celebrating Shabbat, visiting the *mikvah* (ritual bath) or doing the many other mundane things that fill the days of Jews of this kind.

Too Jewish

There are certainly incentives for us to reveal our more dramatic side and play down our everydayness. In April 2024, during the intermediate days of Pesach, the BBC screened a documentary following four British Jewish kids as they prepared for and then celebrated their Bar and Bat Mitzvahs.[8] It was accurate, clear,

respectful and very undramatic. The review in the *Guardian*
newspaper was very sniffy:

> If it was intended as a straightforward documentary for
> adults, it is wildly inappropriately lightweight for the times.
> I would expect such a show to acknowledge many more
> issues and experiences that children – if not these particular
> ones, then others should have been found – are negotiat-
> ing in these increasingly volatile times. To give us this bland
> offering isn't 'wrong' as such. But it is bizarre.[9]

The assumption that a time when Jews are enmeshed in global
drama, a simple documentary about Jewish life must necessarily reflect that, is revealing. It helps to explain why Jews are
tempted into pitching more incendiary fare to production companies. In response to the *Guardian* review, David Chernik, the
Bar Mitzvah DJ featured in the programme, responded in a
warmly appreciative blog post about the documentary:

> Jews alive today only survive because our ancestors man-
> aged to escape at least one genocidal threat over the last 3½
> thousand years. Let's celebrate making it this far. L'chaim!
> (That's the Jewish toast 'to life!')[10]

While there is an unarguable case for the Jewish right to celebrate, focusing that celebration on our 'surviving' still keeps
us yoked to significance. What's wrong with celebrating for the
sake of celebrating?

For all that we are encouraged to lean into our extraordinary side, Jews also worry about being 'too Jewish'. In the
Jewish community in which I was raised we would sometimes
refer to a person more performatively religious than ourselves

as *meshuggenah frum* ('crazy observant' in Yiddish). To be too Jewish doesn't necessarily mean being too observant; it can also mean being too involved in Jewish communal life. To be called a *macher* – a 'doer' who sits on committees and the like – is both to be accorded respect and also to be seen as slightly ridiculous. Having worked professionally for UK Jewish communal organisations since the mid-1990s, I can attest to the constant worry from rabbis and CEOs that the best of our best treat working in the Jewish community as a second-choice career. And having taught at a rabbinic seminary and having been married to a rabbi for over two decades, I can confirm that the joke that being a rabbi 'is not a job for a nice Jewish boy/girl' reflects a real anxiety that devoting one's professional life to doing Jewish might be a parochial dead end.

It's easy to see how accurate depictions of Jewish activities might also be seen as too Jewish. Misrepresentation therefore becomes a way of getting round the inconvenient fact that Jews do a hell of a lot.

Being Jewish is less of a problem. We can be as extraordinary as we wish. We can recite our litanies of woe and angst for public and Jewish consumption. We have become used to Jews in the public sphere who talk about their Jewishness at great length and at every opportunity. The public Jew who does a lot and talks about it publicly too is a much rarer figure. I know some very public Jews who have rarely written anything about the committees I know them to be part of, the voluntary commitments I know them to undertake.

How far can Jewish reticence about Jewish doing be explained by fear of antisemitism? There was a time when it was pretty much irrelevant what you did, to simply be a Jew was enough to damn you. As is often pointed out, the German Jewish population in the 1930s was one of the most assimilated in the world; that didn't save them. Yet while it's understandable that Jews may play down the Jewish way of doing, it doesn't help us when Jews are happy to play fast and loose with the reality of Jewish life.

Christopher Guest's 2006 comedy *For Your Consideration* offers an amusing illustration of these dangers. The film concerns the production of a movie, set in the southern US in the 1940s, called *Home for Purim* and the consequences of a rumour that it would be receiving Oscar nominations. The Jewish festival of Purim commemorates the deliverance of the Jewish people in Persia from the machinations of King Ahashverosh's evil adviser Haman, who wants to wipe them out. Haman's plot is foiled by the Jew Mordechai, via his cousin Esther, whom he manages to marry off to the king. The story is recounted in the biblical book of Esther and scholars have concluded that it appears to bear no resemblance to any historical event.

The production of *Home for Purim* is chaotic and amateurish. The plot of the film revolves around the return of the adult children to the family home for the festival. Dramatic tension is supplied by, among other things, the matriarch of the family's terminal illness and the daughter bringing her girlfriend home. The family's Purim celebration involves a dinner in which they gather in costume to sing a song in English, apparently called 'Purim, Purim, Purim'. The situation is deliberately ridiculous. Purim is not the sort of festival where the members of a Jewish family of the type portrayed in the film would make a special effort to come home for. While the festival is indeed celebrated with dressing up in costume, a special Purim dinner is rarely part of the celebrations; the festival is marked by public festivities, often involving drunkenness, rather than private family gatherings. In the world of *For Your Consideration*, Purim has been misunderstood, deliberately or otherwise, as a Jewish Christmas or Thanksgiving. The festival of Chanukah often performs this function in Christian countries, but never Purim.

Here's the kicker: In the end, the studio producing the film gets cold feet and declares the film to be 'too Jewish' – and so they retitle it *Home for Thanksgiving*. All that effort to bend and twist to accommodate non-Jewish expectations comes to naught. Why have a fictional Purim when you can have the real Thanksgiving?

When Jews hide or downplay the knotty realities of the Jewish way of doing, we imply that all that differentiates us from everyone else is the thoughts that go through our heads and the words that come out of our mouths. However much this kind of Jewish being may be contorted with angst about our place in the world, by ignoring the weight of Jewish doing, we become dispensable and superficial.

The weightlessness of Jewish being leads Jews to conduct another kind of misrepresentation: Desperately scouring the world for the slightest trace of Jewishness and exulting in the crumbs of Jewish existence. This is what I call in the next chapter *Jewification*.

Chapter Three
The Jewification game

You probably won't be expecting this bit
A young Japanese man, wearing a red parka, tours the sites of Sendai, a city in Honshu. At city hall, on a wide boulevard, at a train museum, on a ferry to Matsushima and many other places, he executes an energetic star jump. As if by magic, his trousers and parka fly off his body, leaving him dressed only in a black pair of underpants. Against a pumping dance soundtrack, an excitable commentator announces:

'Broken weeaar!'

The announcements (in a baffling mixture of Japanese and English) follow red parka on his adventures. As he pats an old steam train in his underpants we hear, 'Oh, nice train!'; as he runs towards the camera the announcer proclaims, 'I love you.' Then, after performing multiple broken wears, we move on to a different stunt – Red Parka stands at various spots in Sendai and tips a bucket of water over his head. The commentator exclaims:

'Bucket reverse!'

There's more: I urge everyone reading this to search out the video on YouTube, first posted sometime in the early 2010s.[1]

You will revel not just in broken wears and bucket reverses (including a terrifying 'Black bucket reverse'), but also 'Fire breath', 'Smokey jet' and 'Jumpy jump'. After you have done so, you may continue reading ...

The question you might be asking right now is, 'All very nice, but what does that have to do with Jews?' And that is my question too: Jewishly speaking, what is the significance of Red Parka and his Sendai shenanigans?

At least in its more traditional varieties, Judaism is a total system. It is about the world and all that is in it. Jews are 'chosen' by God to be the people who reflect back the love of God for his entire creation, by observing *halacha,* God's laws for the Jews. Judaism is at once a form of universalism, concerned with 'everything', yet also radically particularist and inward-looking.

Everything has a place in Judaism, even Red Parka. He will certainly benefit from the redemption of the world through the coming of the Messiah, assuming it occurs during his lifetime. He doesn't even have to do that much to receive this bounty, only to keep a limited amount of ethical strictures known as the 'Noachide laws'. Still, in the most stringent forms of Haredi Jewish orthodoxy, Red Parka needs to be kept at arm's length. I don't think that Red Parka would be seen as embodying the most mortal spiritual threat of *avodah zarah* (idolatry, blasphemy, literally 'foreign work'). His partial nudity would certainly be judged inappropriate in orthodoxy, which values *tzniut,* 'modesty' and the restraint of the body, sexualised or otherwise. But even a Red Parka video in which his clothes never fall off would be a problem, not despite but because of its triviality. Such things constitute a *bitul Torah,* a waste of time that would be better spent in study of the Torah and good deeds. Traditionally speaking, then, Red Parka does exist in Judaism: classified and understood as something not wholly benign but not an existential danger; something to be ignored.

Ironically, it is Jews like myself, who do not hold with insular forms of Judaism, who are most likely to claim Red Parka for the Jewish people. It is common for whole swathes of the Jewish people to do the reverse of Haredi Jews, to extend the boundaries of Jewishness as far as possible. This is what I call *Jewification*.

Spot the Jew

If Red Parka was Jewish, I would know. In the years since the video was posted online, my fellow Jewificating truffle pigs would have sniffed him out. We always do. This kind of Jewification – a positive version of the antisemitic witch hunt – seeks to name and highlight Jews in the public sphere. Still, Red Parka, despite starring in a video that went modestly viral a while back, isn't that big a catch. It's the celebrity Jew that scores highest. Adam Sandler's much-loved 'Chanukah Song' 'outs' a grab-bag of names, from Dave Lee Roth to Paul Newman, by way of James T. Kirk and Fonzie. It was the work of the moment for me to find a listicle with some less obvious names:[2] Daniel Radcliffe, Timothée Chalamet, Rashida Jones, P!nk, Drake, Craig David, yadda, yadda, yadda. Jewification tends to measure Jews by weight, the more the better. What's much less clear is what the groaning net full of celebs with some kind of Jewish connection actually *means*. If Red Parka was Jewish, why would it matter?

This is a question I have been struggling with for some years. I am a Jewificator by instinct; I can't stop myself. While watching TV I wonder at the Jewishness of the cast. At the most humdrum of social occasions I find myself looking for signs that any of the people around me are MOT (Member Of the Tribe). I weigh the evidence – the face, the accent, the idioms, the surname – and if I can I share my conclusions with the person in question, whereupon I am often proved right.

I enjoy this game; I also question its purpose. What provoked this questioning was my love of heavy metal music and culture. Since I was a kid my attraction to heavy metal was always tinged with anxiety. In the early 80s, when I fell hard for bands like Iron Maiden, I wondered how I fit into this cheerfully boozy, blokey, blue-collar world. For years I concluded that I simply didn't. But in my twenties, as I embarked on a PhD involving ethnographic research on metal scenes, I began to realise that metal was more diverse than I had previously thought and that this diversity included Jews. There are a fair few Jewish metal musicians; the Wikipedia page on the subject has 72 names at the time of writing and it includes both famous Jews like Gene Simmons from Kiss and Geddy Lee from Rush, as well as lesser-known personal favourites like Josh Silver from Type O Negative.[3] There is also a vibrant Israeli metal scene.

I was happy to find my people in metal. After a while, though, I started to wonder what it all meant. In 2005, the music channel VH1 aired a one-off show called *Matzo and Metal* in which metal Jews like Dee Snider and Scott Ian discussed their Jewish heritage.[4] It was somehow disappointing, despite the novelty of watching the assembled musicians intoning the blessing over the wine and the rest of it. They didn't really have much to say about it all; it was just how they were raised, they felt a certain amorphous pride in it all, but it didn't really impact on their music. If you took the Jewish out of these musicians' lives, would their careers have been any different? Does having a Jewish background matter so much? In a few cases, the Jewish upbringing of some metal Jews has been deeply important, such as David Draiman of Disturbed who had a yeshiva education, Gene Simmons who lived in Israel when he was young, and the members of Anvil, whose close-knit Jewish background helped support them as their career fell apart. For the small number of artists who work with Jewish themes, such as Israel's Orphaned Land, their Jewishness is obviously crucial. For Jewish metal musicians who left their connection to the Jewish community behind in their adolescence and who have little interest in exploring Jewish themes in their work, what real difference does their Jewishness actually make?

In recent years I have started to admit in public – at academic conferences and in my scholarly writing – that Jewish metal may not matter a great deal.[5] It feels thrillingly subversive somehow. When I make that argument I usually have an interlocutor in mind; my sometime collaborator, Professor Nathan Abrams.

Nathan is a professional Jewificator. Much of his work in film studies has involved exploring the hidden histories of Jews on screen and those who make film and TV. Some of his scholarship has been revelatory: His extensive research on the work and life of Stanley Kubrick has revealed that the director's upbringing within the circles of New York Jewish intellectuals played a pivotal part in his artistic development.[6] That kind of Jewification – demonstrating how a person's Jewishness was not incidental to their work, as previously assumed – is one I can definitely get behind. The same is true with Nathan's earlier work on Jewish involvement in the US porn industry, which explored some of the less comfortable aspects of postwar American Jewish sexuality.[7]

Other Jewifications seem less than significant. In 2014, while I was working as the editor of the literary magazine the *Jewish Quarterly*, Nathan approached me with an article he had co-written with Danielle Friel, on the TV series *Sons of Anarchy*.[8] The show, which aired between 2008 and 2014, portrayed the travails of a biker gang called Sons of Anarchy Motorcycle Club Redwood Original (SAMCRO) in Central California. Nathan and Danielle noted the presence of prominent Jewish characters in the show, including one of the bikers and the matriarch of the clan. They also pointed out the Jewish actors, including Ron Perlman as the club president. The article concluded:

> The biker gangs in *Sons of Anarchy* are clearly demarcated along racial lines: there are the Mexican 'Mayans', the African-American 'Niners' and the Neo-Nazi 'NORDICS', all of whom are made of members who belong exclusively to those ethnic groups ... Perhaps in order for our protagonists to appear more sympathetic, SAMCRO had to appear somewhat more multicultural. Including the one excluded minority here, in this case, Jews, was a way of achieving this. Additionally, the inclusion of Jews in a place where they seemingly don't belong goes some way to stretching Jewish televisual stereotypes beyond the Larry Davids and the Jerry Seinfelds, to encompass something broader, more textured, even outlaw.

Although I hadn't then seen the show, the article seemed to make an interesting argument to me so I was very happy to print it. A year or two later I got round to actually watching *Sons of Anarchy*. I kept a close watch out for the Jews and ... I was completely underwhelmed. While the Jewishness of some characters added a bit of colour, you could erase it entirely and the series would be pretty much the same. It seemed to me that the Jewishness on show was a creative choice of little more significance than the colour of a character's hair.

Was I being harsh? I re-read Nathan and Danielle's article and was struck by the following passage about the Jewish character Bobby Munson:

> Interestingly, though Bobby's Jewishness is explicit in this sense, no other verbal or cultural allusions to it are ever made. Bobby is completely assimilated in to SAMCRO, he is a long-standing member (who later becomes vice-president) and is characterised as being extremely tough, often brutal. Thus his Jewishness is never evoked as being a barrier to membership or promotion in a gang in which you simply do not expect Jews to run. In contrast to this, much is made of the black origins of another club member, Juan Carlos 'Juice' Ortiz (Theo Rossi). Juice goes to great lengths to conceal his ethnicity, eventually gunning down a fellow club member who threatens to reveal him. Juice believes that if the club finds out that he has a black father, then his membership and even his life will be in peril. We can calculate, then, that by the club's code, Jews are 'Kosher' where blacks seemingly are not.

To a degree that's a fair argument. It's another example of the ways in which Jewishness is in some contexts today coded as 'white'. The problem is that it finds Jewish significance in its lack of significance. The corollary is that the presence of Jewish characters on TV must always be significant. This doesn't account for the possibility of Jewish irrelevance. Red Parka is intrinsically Jewish because there is nothing Jewish about him.

Over time I have become convinced that we need to make the case for the possibility that Jews in popular culture may sometimes be of only trivial importance at most. There is, in fact, a history of very public and very assimilated Jews proclaiming the insignificance of their Jewishness to the world, as an accident of birth and no more. As the revolutionary Rosa Luxemburg, once famously wrote:

> What do you want with these special Jewish pains? I feel as close to the wretched victims of the rubber plantations in Putamayo and the blacks of Africa with whose bodies the Europeans play ball ... I have no special corner in my heart for the ghetto: I am at home in the entire world, where there are clouds and birds and human tears

The problem is that, until relatively recently, while some Jews might have wanted to unshackle themselves from the weight of Jewishness, it was not their choice alone. The Holocaust engulfed the assimilated too. These days, the heirs of the Jewish radical tradition ironically exult in Rosa Luxemburg, insisting on her radical Jewish significance. That refusal to let Jews be trivially Jewish can be maddening to some prominent Jewish figures. The British Jewish theatre director Jonathan Miller was repeatedly asked in interviews about his Jewishness throughout his life. He was very clear that 'I don't believe in race and I find racial notions so objectionable that I can't think of myself as being Jewish in that way. I'm Jewish for the purpose of admitting it to antisemites.'[9] Still, the interviews and the questions kept coming, often to his irritation, often in the pages of the Jewish media, and after his death in 2019 he was 'rewarded' with a lengthy obituary in the *Jewish Chronicle*.[10]

I am not suggesting that we must always take the claims of Jews who wish to minimise their Jewishness at face value. None of us are completely known to ourselves and one's upbringing and ancestors often exert a force greater than we know. There are also specifically Jewish ways of becoming un-Jewish, what

Isaac Deutscher memorably called the 'non-Jewish Jew', a type whose attempts to distance themselves from the Jewish people are always marked by an ineffably Jewish angst. What I am taking issue with is the obsession that many Jews have with teasing out the gossamer Jewish threads in the biographies of people who are distanced from any kind of Jewish involvement or identification. All too often there is a refusal to accept even the possibility that Jewishness may not mean very much at all. Why shouldn't the non-Jewish Jew be allowed to not be Jewish?

Actually, I would go further: We should consider the possibility that even some of the most explicitly Jewish individuals and cultural works may be less Jewishly significant than we think.

In the previous chapter I showed how Jews sometimes minimise or misrepresent the details of the Jewish way of doing when we present ourselves to the world. What if we turned Jewification and the minimisation of Jewish doing on its head? What if we deliberately sought to *de-Jewify*?

De-Jewification

I've no time for rigid notions of what it means to be 'authentically' Jewish; Jewish culture is just what Jews want it to be, whether I am drawn to it or not. I have no power or desire to police who gets to call themselves a Jew. All that said, we can distinguish between degrees of Jewish commitment and involvement. We can acknowledge that some forms of Jewishness leave a hell of a lot out, to the point of constructing a gossamer-thin kind of flimsiness. The de-Jewification I propose is an attempt to draw attention to what is not there.

Take Leonard Cohen. Yes, that Leonard Cohen, the Jewish singer-songwriter, poet and novelist whose work was imbued with a fascination with Jewish life and ritual. Could you get any more Jewish than 'Who by Fire', his 1974 song that draws on the Rosh Hashanah prayer *Untanneh Tokef*? This prayer (actually a *piyut*, a liturgical poem) recounts the process of judgement that begins on Rosh Hashanah (the Jewish new year) and ends ten days later on Yom Kippur (the day of atonement). The most famous section can be translated as follows:

> On Rosh Hashanah it is inscribed, and on Yom Kippur it is sealed – how many shall pass away and how many shall be born, who shall live and who shall die, who in good time, and who by an untimely death, who by water and who by fire, who by sword and who by wild beast, who by famine and who by thirst, who by earthquake and who by plague, who by strangulation and who by lapidation, who shall have rest and who wander, who shall be at peace and who pursued, who shall be serene and who tormented, who shall become impoverished and who wealthy, who shall be debased, and who exalted. But repentance, prayer and righteousness avert the severity of the decree.[11]

Laughing Len's 'Who by Fire' is oblique and meditative where the original is starkly prophetic. He alludes to fates known and unknown, to those who are destined 'by barbiturate', 'by powder', 'by hunger' and others too mysterious to decode. There is no easy-to-understand 'message' or any clear resolution; just rumination and doubt. It's a masterpiece (if you haven't heard it or read the lyrics, do check them out unencumbered by the inanities of copyright law that prevent me from quoting directly).

But it ain't my *Untanneh Tokef*.

My *Untanneh Tokef* happens at 12.30ish on Rosh Hashanah, just as I am getting tired of the whole thing. I'm uncomfortably dressed in my best clothes and standing up in a vast tent in which my synagogue accommodates the hugely expanded congregation. It's humid and sweaty and, having been there since 10.30 (it would have been earlier if I attended an orthodox synagogue), I am starting to get hungry. And now, at precisely the time that my attention is starting to wander (some have already gone home), is the most solemn, awe-inspiring part of the service. This is not a time for 'happy clappy' melodies, it's a time to bring out the choral big guns. The choir in my synagogue is very accomplished but their skill can leave no place for a Jew in the pew like me. I fidget and feel guilty for my inattention.

When liturgy is prized out of its context, it loses its anchor in the actual doing of Jewish life. Cohen's *Untanneh Tokef* has nothing to do with the experience of the prayer in the messy, uncomfortable reality that is the synagogue. That doesn't make it un-Jewish; after all, Jews have been reworking liturgical texts for millennia, sometimes for the same introspective motives as Leonard Cohen. What it does make it is less 'thickly' Jewish; the words threaten to escape their Jewish grounding and I am sure that many of those who adore the song have little idea of the source material. In short, 'Who by Fire' – and Leonard Cohen – is less obviously Jewish than some would claim. Actually, *this may be why Leonard Cohen was such a great artist.* As I will suggest later in this book, the art that is most thickly embedded in the everyday doing of Jewish life is often the most disappointing art.

Leonard Cohen was easy enough to de-Jewify – after all, poets like him are often too solipsistic to shackle to a collective identity. But what would it be like to de-Jewify someone who is widely understood as the embodiment of a Jewish 'type'? Someone like … Larry David.

De-Jewifying Larry David might seem perverse. Both *Curb Your Enthusiasm* and, before that, *Seinfeld* are suffused with

Jewish characters, situations and tropes. On these shows we visit synagogues, *bris* ceremonies and orthodox Jewish dry cleaners; we witness arguments about antisemitism, intermarriage, the Holocaust and what it is to be a 'self-hating Jew'. David himself seems to talk in the excitable cadences that US Jews are often associated with and peppers his speech with Yiddishisms. His on-screen personality is a *shlemeil*, a *shmuck*; socially, a walking disaster area. He is the embodiment of the great post-war tradition of Jewish comics.

Yet there is also coyness. David's alter-ego on *Seinfeld*, George Costanza, is Italian-American rather than Jewish-American; Elaine often makes clear she isn't Jewish and even Kramer denies he is on one occasion. One way of seeing this is that they are all New Yorkers, and New York is intrinsically Jewish to the point that even the non-Jews are Jewish. Jewification turns an entire metropolis Jewish to the point where Jewishness is everywhere.

Curb Your Enthusiasm is an exploration of the bizarre consequences that follow when Jewishness floats free of the Jew. On *Curb*, this 'Larry David' – so saturated with Jewishness he is almost a synonym for it – frequently offends and angers Jews, having no idea about how to behave in Jewish spaces and no inclination to learn how. At the Holocaust museum he replaces his own soiled shoes with the shoes of a Holocaust victim. He invites a sex offender to his Pesach *seder*. He buys synagogue tickets for Rosh Hashanah from a scalper. On and on it goes.

In *Curb*, Jewish communal life is often portrayed as rigid, pompous and boundaried. But then, so do most of the worlds David passes through. He is an alien everywhere, and while his lack of social skills may sometimes make his life difficult, at other times he relishes the offence he causes. A person who is capable of hiring a prostitute in order to use a car-pool lane, or to set up a coffee shop with the sole intention of annoying a rival coffee-shop owner with whom he has a pointless feud, is so far outside of human norms that he cannot exist within any kind of community. His identifiable Jewish mannerisms and references are but a thin veneer covering a personality that cannot be contained within any one identity, Jewish or otherwise. In fact, the identity that is most apposite for him is that of a rich man who doesn't need to work and is cushioned from the consequences of his ineptitude.

The compulsive social anarchism that 'Larry David' practises is not unique to Jews and it's an open question whether Jews do it in a particularly distinctive way. It's certainly a common trope in comedy. In the UK, the sitcom *Lead Balloon*, which ran between 2006 and 2011 (a period during which *Curb* had yet to have the impact in the UK that it later achieved), explored very similar territory. It was co-written by and starred the comedian Jack Dee as the comedian Rick Spleen. Like David, Spleen is a social disaster area who constantly causes chaos and humiliates himself. True, there are some differences – Spleen is only semi-successful and many of his problems stem from compulsive lying rather than compulsive honesty – but that doesn't mean that David being Jewish and Spleen non-Jewish is necessarily significant. If you look beyond Spleen's downbeat speech patterns and David's excitable ones, what you find is a narcissism and self-indulgence common to both.

Larry David is a very, very funny man and 'Larry David' is a very, very funny character. Most of us – Jews or otherwise – are not very funny. In that respect, *Curb*'s portrayal of Jewish community as straightlaced and humourless does have an unexpected value. As the critic Jeremy Dauber has put it, David's Jewishness is 'an inch deep and a mile wide'.[12] Too often, the 'deeper' forms of Jewish living are portrayed as not having the verve and excitement that Jewificated culture has.

By de-Jewifying Larry David, we can reflect on the costs and benefits of Jewish excellence versus the Jewish everyday.

Are you not entertained?

The de-Jewification process that I am proposing embraces the least exciting cultural virtues: Pedantry and a dull-witted refusal to fall for claims of significance. However absurd it may seem to lean into such unloved tendencies, it helps us expose the greater absurdity. Indeed, Jewificators themselves sometimes acknowledge that Jewification is ultimately absurd. Lenny Bruce's famous 'Jewish and goyish' routine offers this kind of sly acknowledgement, wilfully taunting us with the absurdity that everything in the world is either Jewish or not:

> Kool-Aid is goyish. All Drake's cakes are goyish. Pumpernickel is Jewish, and, as you know, white bread is very goyish. Instant potatoes – goyish. Black cherry soda's very Jewish. Macaroons are very Jewish – very Jewish cake. Fruit salad is Jewish. Lime jello is goyish. Lime soda is very goyish.[13]

The problem is that this game has become so established in Jewish circles, it takes the form of a double bluff, a pretence that we don't actually see the world this way. Here is an extract from one of the many updated homages to Bruce's routine, published in the UK *Jewish Chronicle* in 2023:[14]

> Diet Coke is obviously Jewish
> Full-fat Coke is Goyish, and so is Coke Zero
> Pepsi very Goyish
> Brexit is Goyish
> Easter is Goyish

Christmas is Jewish
Halloween is very Goyish

As a British Jew, I instantly 'get' this list. Diet Coke is the ste-reotypical Jewish pub drink (we are stereotypically not drinkers of pints of warm beer). In the 2016 Brexit referendum, Jews tended to vote Remain, the same as other largely middle-class educated people living in big cities. Easter is much too Christian to be Jewish. Christmas is camp, secular and family oriented, hence Jewish. Halloween is the only false note: We are, after all, the embodiment of evil in many Christian folk cultures, so why not embrace it?

Yet ultimately, the Jewish-Goyish game isn't good for us. How can any reinforcing of stereotypes be good for us? I'm not arguing that these stereotypes necessarily fuel antisemitism; after all, this game usually takes place safely behind closed Jewish doors. No, the danger is that we end up marginalising other Jews, reinforcing a suffocating uniformity. I myself loath Diet Coke. Why should Jews who embrace traditional British pub culture – working-class Jews in particular – be made to feel that there is something non-kosher about it? There were plenty of Jews who voted for Brexit and, however much I might have opposed them, they are part of my community. While I love the Christmas season, many Jews in the UK find it profoundly alienating.

My carping sounds humourless, doesn't it? That's because it is. I offer in my defence an alternative vein of comedy that sati-rises the narcissism of groups who see everything in the world through their own eyes. The Monty Python sketch 'News for Parrots' lampoons those who would see every event as somehow about them ('No parrots were involved today in an accident on the M1'). Another British sketch, 'Ian News' by Stewart Lee and Richard Herring, imagines a world in which people like Ian saw themselves as a significant community that required separate news coverage ('The first news-stroke-magazine made for people called Ian, about people called Ian, made by people called Ian'). Jewish Ians and Jewish parrots could definitely relate to this kind of satire.

I too have played Jewification for laughs. At the Limmud conference in 2019, I organised a show called 'It's the Jewification Game!'. Limmud is a mixture of an educational conference, arts festival and grown-up summer camp, with a playful culture all of its own. The Limmud celebrities who took part in the game had to pick a topic at random from a hat. They then had five minutes to Jewify the topic in front of a panel of judges. They were docked points for negative Jewification (i.e. claiming that the chosen topic was antisemitic) or for lazy Jewification (i.e. connecting a particular Jew to the topic). Most of the topics in the hat were very British, such as: A Cheeky Nando's, *Strictly Come Dancing*, Piers Morgan, Rochdale United Football Club, Hellmann's Mayonnaise, taking the kids to Center Parcs, and so on.

The winner was Rachel Creeger, Britain's only orthodox Jewish female comedian. Her selection was ITV2, the slightly downmarket version of the commercial television channel ITV. Among her arguments was that ITV2 was intrinsically Jewish as British and other Diaspora Jews like adding a second version to things, since we keep a second day of most Jewish festivals.

Although Rachel is a pro, all the panellists made a decent fist of the game; they instinctively knew how to do it. They were happy to throw themselves into the ridiculousness of the game because it wasn't much different from other Jewish games. On the festival of Purim, for example, many synagogues put on *spiels* that retell the story of Purim with knowing references to contemporary popular culture, such as setting the book of Esther in Narnia or Middle Earth. We are trained in *shtick*, in puns and wordplay that re-narrate the world Jewishly.

So broad, long and deep is our tradition that we have the resources to see almost anything through some kind of Jewish lens. It's these resources that Nathan Abrams drew on when, during the 2020 lockdown, I challenged him to Jewify Red Parka. The blog post he came up with made a pretty decent fist of it, for example:[15]

> The first thing to point out is the predominant use of the color red. Along with yellow, red was used to demarcate Jews (e.g. as in Rothschild or 'rothen Schild' meaning 'red sign' in German). We encounter a train, an old loco-motive at that with obvious connotations of the Second World War. The segment on the ferry reminds me of Jackie Mason's quip that the biggest schmuck in the world is a Jew on a boat. Makes me think of the saying, 'Either it's not a Jew, or it's not a boat.' And this character is certainly a schmuck.

As Nathan demonstrated, a people who have been spread across the earth for over 3,000 years is bound to have such a rich historical memory and symbolic vocabulary that, if the will exists, anything can be Jewified. But while Jewification is deeply embedded in Jewish life, it also risks turning Jewishness into a vague state of being rather than something that Jews do. Jewification transforms us into mas-sively important beings while the source of our importance is elided, coming down to existence alone. As Jewification relentlessly spreads, we wither so that only the assertion of Jewish being remains.

The mystery of Jewification

Why do we do this? What are we afraid of? Why do we invest so much effort in deciding whether Diet Coke is Jewish when there is a vast heap of stuff that is unambiguously Jewish? Coke is, in fact, a good example of this perversity. It seems that the specially brewed Israeli version of Coke that is produced without corn syrup so that it is kosher for Pesach isn't worth mentioning. It is definitely worth satirising, since avoiding corn products on Pesach is a stringency based on erroneously treating corn as if it were leavened grain, a dubious tradition that only Ashkenazi Jews bother with.

Do other peoples do this? Do Unitarians and Quakers comb the showbiz world to find anyone with a grandparent who went to a service many years ago? Do Roma debate whether Dr Pepper is the embodiment of their existence rather than Canada Dry Ginger Ale? To be sure, Jews didn't invent parochial myopia. The British sketch show *Goodness Gracious Me* featured a British-Indian character who was convinced that pretty much everything in the world is fundamentally Indian. When his son announces he is converting to Christianity, he is perfectly fine with it, as Jesus was Indian: 'He worked for his father – Indian. His parents had children without having sex – Indian. He fed five thousand people with two loaves and five fishes – Indian picnic.'

When peoples, Jewish or otherwise, desperately seek to find a connection between them and everything in the world, they are denying a terrifying suspicion: The world would carry on fine without us and – even more terrifying – the world would have been fine if we had never existed in the first place. The Jewish encounter with Red Parka opens up an existential abyss: He is not just non-Jewish, he inhabits a space in which Jews are entirely irrelevant. We can attempt to Jewify him as much as we like, but he is impervious to us.

I'm sure that many other peoples share the Jewish anxiety that the world does not need them. Certainly, peoples that have experienced genocide and persecution will have glimpsed this horrific prospect. However, it is possible that the irony of searching for the most ineffable traces of our existence and ignoring the most distinctive stuff is unique to us. Returning for a moment to the argument I made in the previous chapter, it is utterly bizarre that we try so hard to Jewify popular culture and then play down Jewish distinctiveness in a show like *Friday Night Dinner*. Something here needs explaining. As I will argue in the next chapter, the contradiction has a lot to do with an anxiety about Jewish numbers – about how and whether Jews *count*.

Chapter Four

Frailty in numbers

Jews in numbers
How many Jews do you think there are in the world? Or in your country?
    Wrong.

It is common to over-estimate how many Jews there are. For example, one US study in 2022 found that Americans guessed on average that Jews make up 30 per cent of the country's population (the real proportion is about 2 per cent).[1] In the UK, when I teach non-Jews about Jewish life I often ask them to estimate how many Jews live in the country; usually, they guess around a million when the actual number is around 300,000. While it is true that sizes of other minority populations are often overestimated by survey respondents, there is something I find particularly poignant about overestimating how many Jews there are in the world. Because the number of Jews in the world is an anxious topic for many Jews. There just aren't very many of us.

For the record, at the time of writing the latest estimate of the global Jewish population stands at 15,253,500.[2] There is only one country in the world where Jews are in a majority – Israel – and in vast swathes of the world there are virtually no Jews to speak of. Indeed, the twentieth century saw an accelerating process of Jewish disappearance. I am not just talking about the Holocaust here, although of course it had a dramatic effect. There are 4,500 Jews in Poland today; there were around 3 million before the Holocaust. Mass emigration (forced or voluntary) to Israel of entire Jewish populations from the Muslim world after the state of Israel was formed, as well as from the former Soviet Union after the fall of communism, were also dramatic. Jews also disappeared from many areas in a process of consolidation, in which small Jewish communities declined, their members moving to big cities with already substantial Jewish populations. In the US, Jews largely disappeared from parts of the southern states. In the UK, Jewish populations largely vanished from areas such as the Welsh valleys and Wearside. Burgeoning Jewish life in big, cosmopolitan cities was often achieved through migration of young Jews from places like Mobile, Alabama and Merthyr Tydfil, Wales.

I'm not clear whether Jews are, on the whole, any better informed than non-Jews about the actual sizes of Jewish populations. I would hazard a guess that most Jews are unlikely to overestimate Jewish population sizes. Certainly, Jews outside of Israel, and (perhaps) a few US cities like New York, would have no reason to overestimate the number of Jews in the world. In London and the South East, for example, you only need to travel a couple of miles in any direction from the Jewish hotspots of Barnet, Hertsmere and Hackney to find neighbourhoods with negligible signs of Jewish life. We have absolutely no reason to believe that we are anything but a very small sliver of the UK population and a minuscule slice of humanity in general.

You might think, then, that Jews would be desperate to add to their numbers. You might also think that Jews might be quite flattered that we give the impression to the world of being a sizable multitude. Yet the Jewish attitude to counting Jews can be strange and contradictory, shot through with ambivalence. Understanding that strangeness can help us understand how the equally strange phenomenon of Jewification is a paradoxical response to our smallness.

Count it

One of my favourite Jewish hip-hop albums is *Count It,* a 2008 collaboration between rapper Y-Love and beatboxer Yuri Lane. *Count It* is entirely a cappella (although Lane's skills are such that you sometimes forget). It is designed to be played during the period known as the *Omer,* the 49 days between the festivals of Pesach and Shavuot, symbolising the transition between the exodus from Egypt and the giving of the Torah on Mount Sinai. The solemnity of this period is displayed in the observance of a number of mourning practices, including the prohibition on instrumental music. *Count It* makes creative use of this prohibition by featuring no instrumental music at all. The title reflects the fact that Jews do not describe themselves as 'observing' the *omer,* but as 'counting' the *omer.*

Counting is part of other rituals too. The Sabbath and festivals are fixed in an immovable schedule. While you can bring in Shabbat early and finish it late, the core 25 hours cannot be changed. Shabbat and festivals begin at nightfall, traditionally marked by the appearance of three stars in the sky, which of course is a recipe for chaos as, aside from the issue of what to do on a cloudy night, night falls at different times at different longitudes. In ancient times, the rabbinic assembly announced the sighting of the new moon. As Jews spread across the world, the difficulty in disseminating news of the new moon on time led to some festivals being given a second day to 'catch up'. Even today, the traditionally observant have yet to jettison this venerable failsafe for ensuring that Jews everywhere observe festivals on time.

Jews also count to transform the world. The practice of *gematria* assigns numbers to Hebrew letters and uses the results in esoteric divination and speculation. This activity, which has an important place in the Jewish mystical tradition (*kabbalah*), is a dangerous one. Traditionally, knowledge of the kabbalah was restricted to select adepts who could remain Jewishly grounded as the ordered (numbered) world dissolved into the ineffable.

Counting Jews can be a simultaneously sacred and dangerous act. In Genesis 26:4, God makes the covenant with Isaac that 'I will make your heirs as numerous as the stars of heaven, and assign to your heirs all these lands, so that all the nations of the earth shall bless themselves by your heirs.'[3] In Hosea 2:1, the prophet of the same name doubles down on the prediction, 'The number of the people of Israel shall be like that of sands of the sea, which cannot be measured nor counted.'[4] This doesn't seem to have come to pass yet, unless you have a parsimonious view of the number of stars in the sky, the grains of sand on the beach, or you think God is still working on it. Again, there have never been that many of us. This may be one of the reasons why there is a Jewish tradition that Jews should not be counted; if counting Jews is possible, then that is evidence that the covenant is yet to be fulfilled. Still, this taboo does not quite have the status of law, and today most Jews other than those within the most insular sects participate in censuses and surveys.

There is also a tradition that celebrates Jewish multitudes. One blessing I have never recited is the one to be said on seeing 600,000 Jews in one place, 'Blessed are You, Lord, our God, King of the Universe, knower of secrets.' This is a reference to the multitudinous secrets in all of our hearts that only the almighty can know. The blessing is a reminder that, even if we do count Jews, only God can really know them. The blessing itself is taken from the following passage in the Talmud:

> And Rav Hamnuna said: One who sees multitudes of Israel, six hundred thousand Jews, recites: Blessed ... Who knows all secrets. One who sees multitudes of gentiles recites: 'Your mother shall be sore ashamed, she that bore you shall be confounded; behold, the hindermost of the nations shall be a wilderness, a dry land, and a desert.'[5]

In other words, if seeing a multitude of Jews is a cause for a blessing, the multitudes of non-Jews are a reproach, a sign of disfavour. However many Jews there are, we are tiny compared to the rest of humanity.

Counting out

Even if Jews may have been historically reluctant to count themselves, we have been less reticent about *counting out*. We wish to be many, but we are fussy about who can be included in our ranks. That setting of a high bar is embedded in daily prayer services. While solo prayer is allowed and sometimes unavoidable, some prayers can only be recited in the company of other Jews, such as the mourner's *kaddish* prayer. Traditionally, collective prayer requires a *minyan*, a quorum of ten Jewish adult men. There is a vast rabbinic literature on who can make up a minyan and who cannot. We do not make it easy on ourselves. Even progressive Jewish movements who have done away with this requirement still treat collective prayer as the ideal.

Jews also count out by defining Jews by descent alone. For centuries, a Jew has been defined as a person with a Jewish mother. Although Jews who meet this criterion may be counted out of communal life on various other criteria (such as embracing another religion), the definition itself is blind to belief and behaviour. For much of Jewish history, when Jews were forced to live in insular communities, it was usually easy to know who was Jewish. Today, now that Jews have the freedom to live and marry as they wish, things are less straightforward. In recent decades, some progressive Jewish movements have begun to accept children of a Jewish father as Jewish, but that is not the case in orthodoxy. Even Jews who are children of a Jewish mother may not be accepted if that mother's Jewish status could not be proved or they were converted outside of orthodoxy. In Israel, this has led to countless problems when Jews who are considered Jewish by the relaxed rules of the state are not judged sufficiently Jewish by state-run religious authorities. Jewish soldiers who have been killed fighting for Israel have been denied burial in Jewish cemeteries, for example.

Another reason why the Jewish people has stayed small is that Jews refrain from actively seeking converts. While in antiquity there were times and places when Jews sought recruits – if not, how would there ever have been Jews in the world? – in the Diaspora, outreach to non-Jews has often been exceedingly unwise. In Jewish law there is virtually a requirement to discourage prospective converts, at least on their first attempt. There is a famous Talmudic passage which gives the form of words to do this, versions of which have subsequently been adopted in Jewish legal codes:

> If a man wishes to become a proselyte he is not accepted
> at once but they say to him, 'Why do you want to become

a proselyte? Do you not see that this people are debased, oppressed and degraded more than all other peoples, that diseases and chastisements come upon them and they bury their children and children's children, that they are slaughtered for [observing] circumcision, immersion and the other precepts [of the Torah] and cannot hold up their heads like other peoples?'⁶

There are further hurdles too: Tests of sincerity, arduous learning, immersion in the ritual bath and (for men) circumcision. Traditionally, conversion for the purposes of marriage to a Jew does not count as an acceptable motive.

In the modern era, progressive Judaisms have relaxed these constraints. Synagogues may be warm and welcoming to prospective converts, regardless of whether they are converting for marriage. There are courses for converts that take months or a year or two, and don't involve excessive scrutiny and testing. The more pleasant term 'Jews by choice' is now preferred over the more forbidding words convert or proselyte. Nonetheless, 'evangelical' efforts to seek out potential Jew converts are extremely rare and verge on the taboo even in the most progressive Jewish communities.

It isn't just orthodox Jews who express concern about the motives of converts and the impact of having 'too many' of them in the congregation. In 2022, Avitall Gerstetter, the cantor of the progressive Oranienburgerstrasse Synagogue in Berlin, caused a storm of controversy by suggesting that there might be an excessive number of German converts to Judaism. Gerstetter argued that some converts wanted to join the Jewish people for the 'wrong' reasons, such as atonement for the Nazi period, and that the sheer number of converts in some synagogues meant that services felt more like 'an interreligious event'.[7] She was dismissed from her post but her words did strike a chord with some.

The only way to grow if prosleytisation is off the table is to mass produce more Jews. That's what Haredi Jews have done in the post-war period. Having lost so much in the Holocaust, including entire rabbinic dynasties and countless places of learning, the post-war strategy was clear: Have as many children as you can and insulate them as far as possible from outside influences to ensure they don't (or can't) leave. Families of ten or more are common and, although some do drop out as adults, the success of the Haredi rush to procreate is obvious. They do indeed make up a multitude and their quasi-uniform dress (for men) makes this plainly visible. In his ethnography of Haredi life in Jerusalem, Samuel Heilman recounts participating in the funeral procession to the burial of a revered rabbi. Thousands of black-clad followers snaked their way through East Jerusalem to the Mount of Olives where multitudes jostled for a better view of the burial:

> At the entrance to the valley of the shadow of death, quite a few stood on the precipice and stepped back to watch the sea of black flow into the canyon and up the mountain. 'Look, look,' a father said to his children. But it was not just the rabbi's body in white surrounded by the black of the mourners' coats that he pointed out. It was the sight of so many of their own that he showed his children. Out of death came a reminder of life. 'Look how many people, look how many we are!'[8]

Haredi Jews have every reason to celebrate. One recent estimate suggested that they number over 2 million, 14 per cent of the total world Jewish population, and are growing by

3.5 to 4 per cent annually, while the rest of the Jewish world shows a sluggish 0.7 per cent growth rate.[9]

For the rest of us, Jewish social research proves to be an Eeyorish discipline. I should know, having made part of my career in this field. The policy-oriented surveys commissioned by Jewish organisations are diagnostic; they highlight problems and feed worries for the future. In the first few decades of the twentieth century, counting Jews often meant counting *vulnerable* Jews. Jews had always known that they were a scattered and vulnerable people, but the development of modern scientific techniques for counting populations and their characteristics allowed the consolidation of Jewish collective knowledge in piteous detail. Social scientists and demographers associated with the early Zionist movement, such as Arthur Ruppin, used statistics to reveal the 'pathological' nature of Diaspora existence, its poverty and its weakness; Jews were literally sickened by their exile.[10] At times such self-lacerating science came dangerously close to eugenics, to the 'race science' that, while present across political dividing lines in the pre-war period, had catastrophic consequences under the Nazis.

The double-edged nature of Jews counting Jews reached its apotheosis during the Holocaust. The Nazis aimed for total control. There is a well-known statistical table prepared for the January 1942 Wannsee Conference, in which Nazi leaders sought to better coordinate the extermination process that was already under way. The table lists the number of Jews for each European country, including those that were not under their control, coming up with a total number of 11 million.[11]

Such use of numbers is piteously cold, but it becomes even more horrific when we acknowledge that Jews themselves

sometimes played a part in assembling these counts. In Poland
the Nazis developed a sadistically efficient way of controlling
and then eliminating the Jewish population. Jewish leaders
were compelled to form Jewish councils (*Judenräte*) to govern their Jews and, eventually, to administer and police the
ghettos where Jews were confined. A crucial part of the work
of the *Judenräte* was counting who was alive, who was fit to
work and who was fit only for deportation and murder. The
Judenräte were compelled to serve their masters with endless
statistical reports, which required considerable bureaucracy.
In some of the largest ghettos, this forced bureaucratisation
went much further, creating an entire apparatus of statistical
monitoring. As Isaiah Trunk recounts in his classic history of
the *Judenräte*:

> In the Łódź ghetto the statistical office covered almost all
> fields of ghetto administration. It was subdivided into a
> number of divisions: demography, occupations, health,
> welfare, food supplies, courts, security etc. The department
> operated its own graphic and photographic laboratory,
> where 44 persons were employed in May 1944. All depart-
> ments of the ghetto administration were ordered to submit
> reports and statistical data. The statistical office prepared
> statistical yearbooks and anniversary albums, portray-
> ing the activities of the various branches of the ghetto
> administration.[12]

In the Łódź ghetto, the development of such a labyrinthine statistical project was part of a concerted attempt,
under its authoritarian Jewish leader Chaim Rumkowski,
to save its Jews. Rumkowski believed that, by making the
ghetto an efficient hive of industry serving the German war

economy, 'his' Jews could be saved. Statistics were essential to the project of demonstrating, both to the Germans and to the Jews, that the ghetto was efficient, productive and soberly run. Counting Jews in the Łódź ghetto was an enterprise that was simultaneously craven collaboration and an audacious attempt to survive. Counting could even be resistance in some ghettos. Warsaw, the largest ghetto of them all, attracted escapees from labour camps and other ghettos who could not be officially registered. Given that the meagre food supplies the Germans allowed them were based on the official head-count, the *Judenräte* sometimes needed to cook the books.

Statistics could also form a kind of legacy bequeathed from a community facing destruction. In the Warsaw ghetto, a group of doctors led by Izrael Milejkowski conducted a pioneering study on the effects of starvation in 1942, in the final months before the majority of the ghetto was deported to Treblinka.[13] Disaster and chaos was transformed into the immortality of knowledge, displayed in numbers and charts.

In the Nazi period, to be counted as Jewish was a disaster. There was an appalling expansiveness to the Nazi definition of a Jew. It was irrelevant how you defined yourself or even if you had converted. In the Warsaw ghetto there were even churches for the use of Christians who had been consigned to the Jewish category. In the Nuremburg laws, a person with three or more Jewish grandparents was counted as a Jew. The Nazis struggled to define those with a 'lesser' quantity of Jewishness, consigning those with fewer than three Jewish grandparents to various categories of *Mischling* (roughly 'mixed birth'). While in Germany some *Mischling* did survive, as well as some Jews married to non-Jews, in other areas the Nazis conquered, these niceties were not observed.

There is a grim kind of comedy to the bureaucratic forms that Nazi antisemitism took. The desire to exterminate Jews came up against the convoluted question of what a Jew actually was. The certainty of eliminationist antisemitism confronted the slipperiness of human-created categories and the muddle of identity. Even those, Jewish or otherwise, who wish to count Jews for more benign reasons often end up getting ensnared in the same traps, since counting Jews is incredibly difficult and even the most apparently simple counting exercises can end up raising divisive existential issues. Those who still hold to the taboo on counting Jews should take succour in the woes of those who try to do it.

Losing Jews

I began my career as a Jewish social scientist in the 1990s, a time when anxieties over antisemitism and the future of Israel had abated to the point where they could be replaced with other worries. In Jewish policy-making circles in the UK, US and some other Diaspora countries, one of the main concerns was the prospect that Jews would 'disappear', at least outside of the orthodox world. Jewish population estimates seemed to be precipitously declining (in the UK, from about 400,000 in 1945 to about 300,000 in the early 90s). One of the main culprits was seen as intermarriage, Jews marrying non-Jews, losing their Jewishness and producing non-Jewish children. I have recounted the history of British Jewish concerns about intermarriage and attempts to counter the phenomenon in the 2010 book I co-authored with Ben Gidley, *Turbulent Times*. What's important to note here is that the anxiety – even moral panic – about assimilation and intermarriage was often driven by depressing demographic figures and survey results. However much Jewish leaders were desperate to stem the tide, they continued to count Jews out and showed a marked reluctance to commission research on what those Jews who had 'disappeared' actually practised or believed. There was a degree of masochism to the whole exercise.

Social research on Jewish populations has shown that 'feeling' Jewish persists across the generations much longer than 'doing' Jewish does. Intermarriage paradoxically increases the number of Jewishly connected households. Some sections of the Jewish world have tried to see the persistence and broadening of Jewish feeling as an opportunity. In much of the UK progressive Jewish world, it is an article of faith in some quarters that 'if only' we were more welcoming then Jews would be attracted to Jewish communities. Some sections of orthodoxy have developed practices of what has become known as *kiruv* ('outreach'), a kind of internally directed analogue of Christian evangelism, in which dynamic rabbis and teachers attempt to make Judaism attractive to the 'lost'. Even those who 'wrote off' Jews to assimilation in the 1990s did attempt to improve the dynamism of Jewish life, Jewish education in particular, to retain those who were most at risk of disappearance. The net result of these and other initiatives to ensure 'Jewish continuity', as it has become known, is difficult to ascertain.

Today, communal worries have returned to antisemitism and Israel. These require a different kind of counting to address: a whole infrastructure that has been rolled out in multiple communities to count antisemitic incidents, survey the prevalence of antisemitism attitudes in the general population, and measure levels of anxiety about external threats experienced by Jews themselves. High-profile counting exercises such as the ADL Global 100 in the US, which measures the level of antisemitic attitudes across the world, are what stir the blood now.[14]

What has stayed the same is the ambivalent attitude that Jews have to numbers. In particular, while counting Jews obsesses us and scares us, there is a vast amount of Jewish life that is rarely counted. We don't seem to be that interested in counting *things*: organisations, buildings, finances, material culture, the products of Jewish life and Jewish peoplehood. For all the anxiety about the number of Jews, we rarely think to find consolation in the sheer weight of Jewish stuff. While the UK Jewish community has a better record in counting Jewish things than some other Jewish communities, in recent years funding challenges have made it difficult to repeat what were once annual counts of the numbers of Jewish synagogues. It is easier to fund surveys than the dull stuff of communal counting. Elsewhere, there are entire dimensions of Jewish life that are completely uncounted; we do not, for example, even know how many Jewish schools there are in Europe, let alone how many Jewish pupils attend them.

Jews count out more than just Jewish people. Rather than celebrate the multitude of Jewish doing, it seems like Jews prefer to fret over the numerical vulnerability of the Jewish people. For Jews, counting can never be a straightforward activity.

The Jewification solution

There is, though, a kind of Jewish counting that consoles: counting 'on' our *presence* in the world, our impact and our influence. Our presence is counted in the weight of *visibility*. This is an accounting of how far we, as a small people, 'punch above our weight'. We measure our health by our celebrities, our brilliant intellectuals, our businessmen and women, our media-friendly rabbis. Jewification, as I described it in the previous chapter, is part of a whole apparatus of ways in which we can see ourselves in the world. It is a version of Jewish chosenness for Jews who cannot believe in a unique Jewish destiny. It is multitudinousness for Jews who cannot or will not add to the multitude through having huge families. It is Jewish continuity for those who have given up on or find distasteful the idea of endogamy and shunning the intermarried.

While Jews may be keen to identify every trace of Jewishness in the world, we grow justifiably anxious when antisemites do the same. 'Punching above our weight' is but a step away from sinister myths about Jewish control of the media and other professions. And in any case, Jewification can become a treadmill, a continuous and exhausting effort to see ourselves in the world in order to convince ourselves that we matter. David Baddiel's well-known book *Jews Don't Count* provides a useful service in skewering how the left often ignores antisemitism, treating us as too privileged to be of concern. Yet in using the term 'count', and in filling his book with examples drawn from journalism and the media, Baddiel also reveals a deeper anxiety about whether, for all our Jewification, we actually matter.

Jewification rarely sees the everyday, the vast array of the Jewish mundane. Metaphorically and literally, Jews don't count it and don't count on it. The anxieties that lead Jews to assume their presence in the world needs to have an impact and be seen to do so, are understandable ones. Given our history it isn't surprising that many Jews associate insignificance with vulnerability. Sociologically and historically, though, it's an open question whether the survival of a people is dependent on its visibility and 'importance'. Whether or not our public presence helps ensure our survival, there are definite downsides to a people that is continually and anxiously looking outward.

Jewification leads us to misrepresent ourselves to ourselves; it implicitly denigrates everyday Jewish doing.

What if Jews didn't have to count? What if we were to embrace *in*significance? What if we were to accept our small numbers and not seek to artificially inflate our presence through Jewification? In the next chapter I suggest that Jews should go for quality rather than quantity – *low* quality, in fact.

Chapter Five
Punching below our weight

The horror, the horror

One night in December 2023, during the festival of Chanukah, my son did a valuable service for the Jewish people.

An undergraduate student at a British university, he has followed a similar path to my own: Having attended a Jewish school all his life (just like I attended a school where around half of the pupils were Jewish), he wanted to discover the wider world. The core of his university social life is bracingly Jew-free, as was mine. Just like me, though, he still feels the need to explain what it is to be a Jew. Unlike me, he found a way of doing it that represents a major contribution to interfaith understanding.

One night during Chanukah, he invited his friends to his room to share candle lighting, apricot brandy and supermarket doughnuts. By all accounts it was a convivial evening. Clearly, my son was relaxed enough to share one of the deepest secrets of the Jews ...

They're called the Maccabeats.

A bunch of peppy, preppy orthodox Jewish young men who met at Yeshiva University (a predominantly orthodox institution based in New York), they are an unavoidable presence in the social-media feeds of anyone even faintly Jewish. The Maccabeats are famous for their unfunny parodies of pop hits, and almost every year they release a new one to coincide with not-Christmas. The video my son showed was from 2010, the year they burst onto the Jewish scene. 'Candlelight' is a semi-a-cappella borrowing of Taio Cruz's hit 'Dynamite', with a toe-curlingly painful chorus that celebrates flipping latkes in the air and spinning their dreidels.[1]

Many Jews I know *love* the Maccabeats. However much I think they represent a watering down of everything that makes pop music exciting, however much I loathe their clean-cut sincerity, however much I am revolted by the very concept of using pop hits for the purposes of 'outreach', and however much the lyrics are unfunny and obvious, nothing I say is going to change the fact that my timeline will be full of reposts of Maccabeats videos every bloody Chanukah from now until the earth cools.

Still, the Maccabeats can perform a useful service to non-Jews. They demonstrate that Jews are capable of producing art that is mediocre or just plain bad.

By all accounts, my son's friends were amused, horrified and enthralled by the Maccabeats, so he kept going. He tapped into the rich vein of excruciating Jewish rap, revealing to the non-Jewish world specimens such as Antithesis, The Zionist Rapper. A British ex-leader of a Zionist youth group, Antithesis struck upon the genius idea of mixing hackneyed pro-Israel slogans (e.g. 'Yes to peace, no to terror') with the occasional 'Do you know what I am saying?' and – hey presto! – Zionist rap.

Perhaps wisely, though, my son decided that his friends were not ready for Etan G, The Jewish Rapper. His 2002 album *South Side of the Synagogue* contained the classic 'Making the Motzee', a rap about how great it is to make the blessings over Shabbat dinner, 'kickin' the kiddush' over the wine and so forth. Etan G is on a mission to make Judaism cool for young people alienated from Jewish life. I'm sure that using terms like 'kickin' the kiddush' will solve the assimilation crisis.

Like my son, I have a passion for sharing mediocre Jewish music with the wider world. At academic conferences and lectures I was, for a time, almost evangelical about demonstrating how, among our own kind, Jews are capable of wallowing in the aesthetic swamp. I still feel that same enthusiasm; this was one of the book chapters I was most looking forward to writing. However, as I will explain, my attitude to mediocre Jewish music has shifted. Without ever coming to like it, I have come to feel a strange affection for it. I now believe that mediocre Jewish music can perform a vital service to Jews and non-Jews, not despite it being mediocre but *because* it is mediocre.

The kind of Jewish music that I am talking about here is quite specific: English-language (and often American) Jewish music that has a 'parasitic' relationship to its parent genres; appropriating, pastiching and parodying. Artists who make this music are motivated by a desire to make Judaism more attractive and relevant to the modern world. Hey, kids – Judaism can be cool, daddy-o!

While Jewish rap is a particular fascination of mine, I also have an obsession with the music of progressive Jewish movements, often born in US summer camps, that has made significant inroads in progressive synagogues around the world. During the 1960s and 70s, this was a daring and even revolutionary development. It seems hard to believe now, but the likes of Joan Baez and Peter, Paul and Mary – who formed the template for Jewish summer camp music – were once radicals, aesthetically and politically. The most influential Jewish musician of this type was Debbie Friedman. Until her death in 2011, she contributed many settings of prayers to the Jewish liturgy, some of which even made it out of the progressive world into orthodoxy. Her most famous work, 'Mi Shebeirach', a healing prayer, is now an established part of the liturgical canon. She earned and deserves her place in Jewish history as the first woman (and an LGBT woman at that) to make such a contribution to Jewish prayer; having met her twice I can also confirm she was a lovely person. She also wrote songs that were designed more for performance and listening than worship. This side of her repertoire comes across like a pallid version of obsolete popular styles. The recorded version of one of her most popular songs, 'And the Youth Shall See Visions', whose title comes from Joel 3:1, is drenched in sappy strings and sappy lyrics (e.g. 'We must live for today, we must build for tomorrow'). Like much of her English-language work, the wondrous complexity of Jewish text and Jewish language is reduced to easily digestible upbeat messages.

This bare-bones description may seem vaguely familiar to some readers. Yes, it also describes contemporary Christian music. While the Jewish musicians I describe aren't seeking to evangelise to non-Jews, they are often seeking to encourage greater religiosity or at least religious participation, particularly among Jewish youth. The performative emphasis on 'feeling it' and trite, simple messaging is another point of connection to contemporary Christian music. Sometimes when I hear contemporary Jewish music I feel like praising Jesus.

I'm not being very nice here, am I? I do know better. My intellectual training taught me that there are no absolute standards of aesthetic judgement and my experience as a researcher has taught me to be magnanimous about the idiosyncrasies of taste. Nonetheless, I do think that the judgement of 'mediocrity' is defensible. The kind of contemporary Jewish music I have described here is based on an appropriation from other genres, sometimes for instrumental ends, without any intention of contributing to those genres. It only replicates, usually in such a way that blunts the rough edges of the parent genre. It depends on its audience suspending or compromising their wider musical preferences and their capacity for judgement. This is music that only has a value because it is tied into explicitly Jewish settings, practices and institutions. The question is whether any of this constitutes a 'problem'.

Learning to love Jewish musical mediocrity

A few years ago, appalled fascination drew me to a performance by the American artist Rick Recht at the annual UK Limmud conference. Recht, often described as a pioneer of Jewish rock, is a regular on the summer camp and synagogue circuit. That night Recht, his acoustic guitar and his almost apologetically quiet rhythm section were inspirational, oh-so-very inspirational, hands-in-the-air inspirational. They played songs of hope, of healing, of inspiration (did I mention that?) ... The audience sang, sang, sang and were inspired.

I spent much of the show venting *sotto voce* to my long-suffering wife about how awful Recht was. Tellingly, I was talking too loudly and disturbed the guy in front of me, who angrily shushed me. That's not something that would have happened at a Motörhead gig. I had known the annoyed one for years, and I remembered having a long conversation with him at a previous Limmud about music and how he booked rock bands while a student. We had some musical common ground in alternative acts of the 80s. And now he was being inspired by the kind of artist that he would have ridiculed if it wasn't for the fact that Recht tossed the odd Hebrew phrase into his lyrics instead of mentioning Jesus.

My outrage crystallised into angry conviction: People like Rick Recht were turning Judaism into a place where aesthetics take a holiday, a place where the normal rules of taste were suspended. They were teaching Jews to expect second best.

Somewhere along the line, though, I began to rethink my obnoxious sanctimony. Well, a bit, anyway. The key factor was my children. Sometimes, round the family dinner table, we end up getting our phones out and entertaining each other with the bizarre, cringeworthy and wonderful dregs of YouTube. That has included me regaling my kids with the horrors of the Maccabeats and worse. Eventually, I realised that we were having an enormous amount of fun. This might not have been the sort of fun that the Maccabeats would like us to be having, but I began to feel a kind of affection for them. I started to wonder *what was so terrible about Jews taking aesthetic holidays?*

I could certainly use such a holiday. To be Jewish today is a heavy, heavy thing. To be so publicly visible can be a burden and that burden is made heavier if we expect our culture to be extraordinary, excellent and important. Maybe the post-1960s growth of Jewish popular music of the kind I am talking about can partially be explained by a desire not to have to try too hard anymore. In the progressive Jewish world, it is striking how the liturgical music that developed in the nineteenth century struggled mightily to equal the glories of the most grandiose kinds of church music, complete with choirs, organs and allusions to high art. In contrast, the music that was born out of Reform summer camps from the 1960s onwards isn't just much simpler to play, it's also more modest in its aspirations. It may sound like 60s US folk music much of the time, but it is never impolite enough to add the edge that Bob Dylan had. It knows its place.

My frustration at Jewish music that didn't seem to aspire to much was misplaced, *as that is the whole point*. To judge it by wider standards makes no sense. It's as ridiculous as if I were to turn up to a school show and expect a Schoenberg recital or a Beethoven symphony. As a parent I have attended countless school shows and I cared about their 'quality' only to the extent that my kids felt content with their performance. Insofar as Jewish communities sometimes feel like extended families, there is a value in taking aesthetic holidays and relaxing into the closeness of my people. If my people perform mediocre art, that's because all but a tiny minority of humankind is mediocre.

Mediocre Jewish music is also a riposte to Jewification and the characterisation of the likes of Leonard Cohen as Jewish artists. The Maccabeats and Rick Recht are not more Jewishly authentic, but they are more Jewishly embedded than more celebrated Jewish artists. Their music isn't about their solipsistic quest to satisfy their muse. They have sacrificed art for a greater good, something bigger than themselves. In a way their low aesthetic standards are a sign of their integrity. In contrast, the more that celebrated Jewish artists 'transcend' their connection to Jewish life the more they are celebrated for it. The Maccabeats will never appear in lists of Top 100 albums of all time. The Maccabeats and their ilk are ours as we are theirs.

I am sure some Jewish readers will be a little hurt, or a lot hurt, by what I have written. Some Jews do believe that the artists I've mentioned make an important contribution to Jewish civilisation. Fair enough. Where I am not going to yield is the plain fact that Jewish things can be mediocre. It would be weird if they weren't, but then we Jews are viewed weirdly and that impacts on how we view ourselves. Even if you think I have been unfair on particular aspects of Jewish taste in this chapter, if you feel my examples are poor ones, that's fine; other Jews can come up with their own. It will do us all good. And it will get easier with practice.

But wait ... For all my newfound generosity of spirit, I am playing a dangerous game. Acknowledging that there is a deep vein of mediocre Jewish culture risks validating a certain kind of antisemitic canard. One of the biggest challenges for antisemites in the nineteenth century and beyond has been to account for the inconvenient fact that, once emancipated, Jews immediately began to play prominent roles in the arts. Did this mean that Jews were as talented as everyone else, as deserving of a place at the aesthetic table as anyone else? The only way to resolve the problem was to deride Jewish art as nothing more than crude mimicry; lacking the soul and the rootedness in the *volk* that true art requires, Jews created a simulacrum of art, with nothing to ground it on. At least this was the kind of argument made by Richard Wagner, among others.

See the problem?

To acknowledge Jewish mediocrity would seem to resurrect a poisonous trope. No wonder Jews are so keen to keep the Maccabeats entirely for ourselves! Still, I think we have to be brave here. Hiding our mediocrity condemns us to the drudgery of excellence. It makes us less than human, since the culture that humans create is always going to be a mixed bag. That the same civilisation can give to the world Bob Dylan, Gustav Mahler, and Uncle Moishy and the Mitzvah Men only demonstrates the many different notes that the Jewish orchestra can strike. What's the problem with that?

So I was proud of my son for exposing his friends to the Maccabeats and their ilk. They learned, as few non-Jews ever do, that behind closed doors, we can be human too.

When and where should we be mediocre?

While Jewish mediocrity might be fundamentally normal, that isn't the end of the story. What is the right balance between

Jewish mediocrity and Jewish excellence? When and where should we take our holidays from the extraordinary, and when and where should we work overtime to avoid it?

It isn't always predictable when, where and why Jews settle for mediocrity. You would think that, for example, given how benedictions over wine are central to many Jewish rituals, we would use only the finest vintages. It's not unknown to do so, but it's not common either. The standard type of wine for Jewish ritual occasions tends to be red, cloyingly sweet, with no information on its year of production; an undistinguished syrup at best. And yet, the brands that are used, such as Manischewitz in the US and Palwin in the UK, attract fierce loyalty and even love. I myself love to tell the tale of why Palwin (which is short for 'Palestinian wine' and dates back to the late-nineteenth century) comes in three varieties that no one has ever been able to tell apart, numbered 4, 4a and 10. The story goes that they were the bus numbers in front of Palwin's London offices; this might even be true. While I love the story and Palwin's treasured place in British Jewish culture, the fact remains that the wine is undrinkable in anything other than homeopathic doses. In my house we bless the wine over twenty-year-old sweet sherry. This may be delightful to imbibe but really we are missing the point. When Jews drink terrible wine on sacred occasions it may well be because those wines are comforting in their familiarity and lack of pretension.

Jewish taste, in the literal sense, is often deliberately skewed towards comfort and quantity rather than quality. While Jewish food is a Jewish obsession, there is more to Jewish food culture than taste alone. I'm an Ashkenazi Jew, a descendant of Jews who derive from Central and Eastern Europe, and it is 'my' cuisines that much of the world associates with Jews. While I love bagels, chicken soup, cholent and gefilte fish, I don't have any illusions about where we stand on the global gustatory pecking order. I suspect that Ashkenazi Jews looked at the food of their non-Jewish neighbours and surgically removed the best bits. On my Poland trip discussed in Chapter One, I sometimes felt that the restaurants we ate at were mocking us by demonstrating that Polish food can do vegetables – salads, even! – and multiple other tempting dishes. I wonder just what Polish Jews forgot on the boat over to New York or London.

Jewish law has had a major impact on Jewish food culture. The rigour and punctiliousness of the laws that define what makes food kosher mean that, for those who keep to these laws, it is difficult if not impossible to share in food made by non-Jews. On top of that, in some Haredi communities there are norms against being seen to adopt other cultural practices; even strictly kosher sushi might be viewed with suspicion in some quarters. Add to that a history of antisemitic separation of Jews and non-Jews, and it becomes easier to understand why Polish-Jewish food and Polish-Christian food are not the same thing, even beyond the exclusion of pork and shellfish.

Jewish dietary laws – however strictly interpreted – should not impact on the quality of Jewish food. Pork and shellfish are not essential requirements for dishes that delight the senses. While kosher slaughtering and preparation of meat does have some impact on flavour, since salting and removing the blood has consequences, a decent cook can work around them. Yet the observance of Jewish dietary laws often leads to an inattention to subtlety and flavour, even if it doesn't have to. For example, in kosher restaurants in Israel, the prohibition on mixing meat and dairy produce has had bizarre results. It's easier for restaurants to only serve food that may contain dairy produce or food that may contain meat (both may serve *parev* food that contains neither) and to be certified for one or the other.

But dairy restaurants in Israel often seem to take it as mandatory to slather everything in cream or cheese sauces, smothering them in fatty flavourlessness.

The challenge of separating dairy and meat has also resulted in the creation of a whole range of parev products that can be used in everything. While it's true that this has resulted in considerable innovation (parev ice cream is surprisingly palatable), it has also had an impact on flavour and texture. Parev spreads, used instead of butter, are famously mediocre, leading a disappointing taint to foods cooked in them. In the UK at least, while Jewish bakeries may produce excellent pastries and breads, you really don't want to touch the cookies: there is a reason why butter cookies are made with butter. The dryness of parev cookies almost causes one's mouth to shrivel up.

Jewish taste, or at least Ashkenazi Jewish taste, seems to bend towards a strange desire to *feel* that one is doing Jewish by eating food that is less delightful than it could be.

That weird kind of asceticism even applies to Jews who don't keep kosher. As with many non-orthodox Jewish households, I grew up in a family that took the Pesach dietary restrictions more seriously than the everyday restrictions. That meant that we didn't just avoid bread, pasta, vinegar, beer or the other products containing leavened foods. We went further, observing the Ashkenazi custom of not eating *kitniyot*, pulses, beans or other grains that swell up in a yeasty manner. Our house was filled with awful kosher for Pesach versions of mayonnaise, ketchup, cookies and much else. It was as though on Pesach we were commanded – by a God whose laws we only sort of observed – to mark the exodus from Egypt with substandard ingredients. It would have been perfectly possible to observe even the strictest customs without resorting to dodgy mayonnaise. But perhaps it wouldn't have *felt* like it was Pesach. In a sense, then, Jewish food culture has an almost self-sacrificial element to it; Jewish food can be food that isn't as good as it could be.

Another issue with major consequences for the state of Jewish food is Shabbat. Cooking hot food from scratch is prohibited over the Sabbath, but keeping food warm is allowed. This constraint has led to a particular kind of cuisine to develop. Shabbat dinner on Friday night can be cooked fresh and consumed soon after night falls (although Friday evening synagogue services often mean that dinner will be eaten an hour or two into Shabbat). Lunch on Saturday needs to either be cold or kept on a hotplate. This has resulted in a galaxy of warmed-over dishes – stews, soups and bakes – the most famous being the Ashkenazi staple *chulent*, a bean-based stew with the constituency of wallpaper paste. Such stick-to-your-ribs dishes aren't just required 52 weeks per year, many festivals also have restrictions similar to Shabbat. In the Diaspora, it's not uncommon for two-day festivals to follow or precede Shabbat, requiring three days of hotplate subsistence.

The place that warmed-over food has in the Jewish collective memory and palate has been reinforced by the important place that institutional cooking – and buffets in particular – has in post-war Jewish culture. Summer camps and educational tours play a central role in Jewish socialisation and buffet dining is inevitably the most efficient way of feeding the masses. Organised tours of the state of Israel often encounter the gastronomic culture of the *kibbutzim*, where collective buffet dining was historically the preferred way to eat.

Warmed-over food is therefore associated with peak Jewish experiences – rest, celebration, travel, friendship and fun – and this has consequences for Jewish taste. While it's not necessarily true that it leads Jews to not tell good food from bad, it certainly creates an expectation that joyful food is mushy food.

As with Jewish music, I fully accept that my take on Jewish food culture won't be shared by everyone. Even if you regard the hotplate as the gateway to a palace of earthly delights, it would still be hard to argue that subtlety, freshness and innovation have been prioritised in Ashkenazi Jewish cooking.

And what's wrong with that?

Nothing. Nothing at all.

Jewish mediocrity is, more often than not, the result of prioritisation of other things. When Jews are a bit crap, it's often the result of a more-or-less conscious choice to accept less than the best in favour of something that is considered more important. That leads to an odd situation in which mediocrity can be a sign of vibrant Jewish existence.

Collapsing Jew buildings

While I am wary of Jewish pride, I make at least one exception: I am proud of how most Jewish communal buildings in the UK are mediocre buildings.[2]

That is certainly a lesson I learned from my own Jewish upbringing. The *shul* (Yiddish for synagogue) I grew up in had been founded in the early 70s in what was then a small Jewish community, located just outside of London. We met for years in an underused church in Bushey. Then we bought our own building; another church, another monument to the decline of home counties Christianity, this time on Radlett high street. We worshipped to the musty smell of ecclesia, cut with the odour of Palwin. Until we grew to the point where we could afford to refurbish the place, everything felt decrepit and abandoned. When I absolutely had to visit the toilet I opened the door with my shirt cloaking my hand and pulled the chain with the tips of my fingers (turning on the taps to wash my hands was too icky to contemplate).

When we streamed out of shul, we were assailed by the enticing smell of Chinese food from the restaurant next door. A taunt of sorts, especially on Yom Kippur.

We were ecumenical in our colonisation of Christian space. Sunday morning *cheder* (religion school) was held in a Catholic girls' school, run by nuns from the next-door priory. The building, a maze of towers and corridors, smelled of decay and Sunday dinner. Roast meat and boiled vegetables, prepared in a kitchen we never saw, sustained the similarly invisible nuns and the odd tramp.

The Judaism of my youth was a sensory assault. Everything seemed to be decayed and tattered. To be Jewish meant avoiding the piss on the floor of the toilets of a boarding school in Cumbria where my summer camp was held. To be Jewish meant screaming with fright as cockroaches scuttled across the floor of our holiday apartment in Herzliya Pituach, a then-ragged seaside town north of Tel Aviv.

The senses can deceive. What I smelled, tasted and touched was growth and vitality, built on an insouciant neglect of the material. Our community attracted young and dynamic rabbis, keen to innovate in gender equality. Material comfort was subordinated to growth, commitment and participation. The same was true in the Israel we visited on holiday and the summer camps on which I was a (sometimes) willing participant.

Things have improved. The synagogue I grew up in was eventually refurbished and proved an acceptable venue for my wedding ceremony. When I attend Jewish conferences I stay in hotels that don't have piss on the floor. Experience taught me that not all Israeli holiday apartments are infested with cockroaches. And the musty smell of churches has become a comforting Christian odour once more; the odour of underuse far preferable to the militantly packed pews of a US-style megachurch.

I have certainly been to some beautiful synagogues in the US, where my wife grew up. They do not smell musty and it is a pleasure to attend services in them. I wonder what these buildings do to the Jewish experience, though. Are beautiful buildings that smell nice and look wonderful antithetical to the building of a place that feels like home?

There is certainly a vein of Jewish tradition that accepts mediocre Jewish space with alacrity. Here is one of my favourite Jewish jokes on the subject:

A man comes to his rabbi and asks, 'Every year when I build my *sukkah* [a temporary structure built during the festival of *Sukkot* to commemorate the bivouacs that the children of Israel lived in during their wanderings in Sinai], it falls down immediately afterwards. How can I build a *sukkah* that will stay up?'

The rabbi responds, 'Look at this passage in the Talmud which tells you how to build a *sukkah*. Follow it exactly and everything will be fine.'

The man goes home and builds his *sukkah*, following the instructions in the Talmud to the letter. As soon as he finishes, it falls down.

The exasperated man goes back to his rabbi and tells him, 'Rabbi I did everything exactly right and yet my *sukkah* still fell down! Why did this happen?'

The rabbi takes out the relevant volume of the Talmud and looks at it closely. After a few minutes of intense study he exclaims, 'Aha!'

'Rabbi, what's the answer? How do I keep my *sukkah* from falling down?'

The rabbi replies, 'Yes, Rashi asks the very same question.'

Rashi was the great medieval sage whose pithy genius for clarification is such that, today, his elucidations are printed in a special script on the inside column of a page of the Talmud, closest to the binding, so that if the pages fray, it's the last thing to get damaged.

Still, his glosses on the text can be gnomic or confusing. That's fair enough; the Talmud is a wondrous mess of baffling redactions of complex arguments between ancient rabbis, interspersed by stories whose point is unclear and legal decisions whose basis is obscure. It's quite likely that Rashi winged it when he built his *sukkah* each year. His day job was as a wine merchant. I've always wondered how he managed to balance the requirements of business with his more celebrated career. Maybe he wasn't a very good wine merchant. Maybe he fobbed his buyers off with the equivalent of Palwin or Manischewitz. He was certainly rooted in the world, with its endemic not-particularly goodness. If the fictional instructions on how to build a sukkah didn't work, he would have said so and he would also have continued to glory in them, as an intrinsic part of the great work of ancient rabbinic Judaism.

Jews often stick with ineffective solutions to forgotten problems; we are stubbornly loyal to the sub-par. This is a strain of modern Jewish culture that often goes unnoticed and unrecorded. The extraordinary achievements that Jews have made in the modern world have been accompanied by an undertone of secret mediocrity. In a world that demands we be extraordinary, there is a subversive value in clinging to the second-rate. Yet the most visible Jews are, almost by definition, rarely mediocre Jews. They usually lack the stomach for subversive mediocrity, even assuming that they recognise it exists. So the only way we seem to publicly acknowledge Jewish mediocrity is through jokes and asides. Self-deprecating stereotypes of the Jews' supposed klutzy lack of practical skills abound. In *Friday Night Dinner*, people who work with their hands and come round to fix things are known as 'men'; Jews are never men. While this stereotype is highly dubious (I know two Jewish plumbers), it does at least allow Jewish mediocrity to be acknowledged.

I myself have experimented with public acknowledgement of Jewish mediocrity. In the autumn of 2022, Sukkot celebrations in the UK were made very challenging due to a huge storm, with torrential rain and gale-force winds. That meant that many of the actual Sukkot were destroyed. As Jews gathered miserably in the ruins, I decided to mark this very British Sukkot by collecting some of the photos friends had posted online of their forlorn sukkah ruins. I published them on the website I co-edited, JewThink.[3] It made me smile and raised some gentle laughs. There was no false comfort of Jewification here, no hyperactive insistence on our importance. A broken, poorly erected sukkah is a reminder that what we lack in numbers, we also lack in excellence – and that's absolutely fine.

Chapter Six

Living and dying to organise

Feeling and doing in a time of crisis

So far in this book I have tried to reveal the ways in which Jewish life can be misrepresented and misunderstood by Jews and non-Jews. I have also questioned whether the seriousness, the world-historical importance and the omnipresence that Jews are accorded is actually good for us. Instead, I have suggested that Jews need to treasure everyday Jewish life with all its triviality and endemic mediocrity. We should exult in mundane doing rather than the public performance of angst.

Still, I don't want to suggest that Jewish being and Jewish feeling is irrelevant. Nor do I want to imply that the Jewish experience of trauma is something we should ignore. Jews do feel. And during times of crisis we emote, we express, we rage, we mourn and we lament.

Since 7 October 2023, Jews have been feeling; there's been a lot to feel. The incursion by Hamas and other Palestinian fighters into southern Israel was a profound shock. While some anti-Zionist Jews were shocked with joy at this audacious attempt to temporarily 'return' (at least until the casualty reports came in, and some not even then), most Jews felt the shock of horror, dread and confusion. The civilian casualties and hostage taking was horrible to behold, particularly for Israelis and the many Jews who have connections to Israel. The war that followed and the horrendous suffering of Palestinians in Gaza sparked a kaleidoscopic set of reactions, depending on what kind of Jew you were: Disgust, joy, foreboding, discomfort … You name it, we felt it. And we still feel it.

Feeling is not simply an internal process, a reaction in the heart to external events. When an entire people feels, it does not take the insubstantial form of a fog of gloom that surrounds our collective body. Feeling takes material form; it is reproduced in practice, in doing things that impact on the world about us.

It's no surprise, then, that within a few days, weeks or months of 7 October 2023, a host of new Jewish organisations and projects popped up throughout the world.

Some of these projects sought to memorialise those who were killed and kidnapped. For example, the USC Shoah Foundation, which was established by Steven Spielberg in 1994 and has recorded and archived an enormous body of testimony from Holocaust survivors, embarked on a new project to record the testimonies of survivors of the 7 October attacks.[1] The National Library of Israel also announced a project to serve as the repository for documentation of the event and its aftermath.[2]

Many Jewish leaders in the Diaspora sought to deepen solidarity with Israel in the aftermath of 7 October. That included vigils for the hostages, solidarity rallies and small-scale projects. JW3, London's Jewish community centre, created the 'Lovelock Hostage Bridge', in which Jews were encouraged to add padlocks to the causeway into the venue as a way of showing love and solidarity with the hostages.[3] The Israeli Foreign Ministry set up a scheme for Diaspora communities to 'adopt' towns that had suffered in the 7 October attacks.[4] In France, the Collectif 7 Octobre was created in order to publicise the fate of the hostages and memorialise the 7 October victims.[5]

Ambitious new global organisations, some of which were planned before 7 October 2023 found new urgency to launch in the aftermath, such as the Z3 Project and Global Jewry, deepening solidarity between the Diaspora and Israel.[6] Other projects sought to give Jews a voice for their anxieties, such as Writing on the Wall, a 'new place for expression, creativity and community' which boldly announced 'We will NOT be silent'.[7] Many existing Jewish communal organisations focused on defending Israel and fighting antisemitism, including new coalitions such as the 10/7 Project in the US.[8]

Of course, significant numbers of Jews, in Israel and the Diaspora, opposed the war in Gaza that followed the 7 October attacks, or at least the manner in which it was conducted. The last couple of decades have seen the emergence of a vigorous Diaspora Jewish 'Israel-critical' left that includes Jews who oppose at least the Occupation and sometimes the Zionist project in its entirety. Naturally, that opposition has taken the form of institution building, with organisations such as J Street, Jewish Voice for Peace (both in the US), Yachad, Na'amod, and Jews for Justice for Palestinians (all three in the UK), offering an outspoken alternative to 'mainstream' Jewish support for Israel. In the wake of 7 October 2023, such organisations often provided the spine of a sizeable 'Jewish bloc' on pro-Palestinian demonstrations, although some did prefer to demonstrate separately in order not to be associated with the most vociferous anti-Zionist elements of these demonstrations.

In Israel itself, by the time the attacks took place the country had already been convulsed for several months by massive demonstrations called by a coalition of civil society organisations against the far-right Netanyahu government, particularly against the plan to 'reform' the independent judiciary. After 7 October these networks of protest turned on a dime and refocused on providing aid to displaced families in the north and south of the country. At the more liberal end of the spectrum, new projects and organisations sprung up to try and ensure that, at the very least, tensions in Israel between Jews and Palestinian citizens of Israel were not exacerbated by the war. One new 'grassroots movement', Standing Together, sought to bind Israelis and Palestinians in the struggle for social and economic justice since, as they put it, 'where there is struggle, there is hope'.[9] Standing Together seeded 'Friends of' organisations in the Diaspora too, including multiple branches in the UK.

A more modest way of organising was corralling signatories for the numerous petitions and open letters that have been issued from every point on the Jewish political spectrum. For the most part, the effectiveness of such actions is short-term at best and most do not aspire to more than stating 'here we stand'. Some are more ambitious, though, and aim at catalysing something more substantial. The liberally minded 'Our Jewish Values' statement, released at the start of November 2023 and organised by a coalition of UK progressive Jewish rabbis, was 'shaped based on the voices and work of Israelis – Jewish and Palestinian citizens – who even now are working for safety, justice and freedom for all'.[10] A website was swiftly built to house resources and learning materials.

The reason I have devoted space to this flurry of organisation is not because it has necessarily changed anything. Indeed, it's likely that, in the intervening period between submitting the manuscript of this book and publication, some of these projects will wither or die. There's certainly lots of duplication of existing efforts, sucking up resources that may be better spent elsewhere. To point to this, though, is to misunderstand why and how Jews organise. The model of institution building that carefully pinpoints an unmet need, carefully consults with stakeholders and carefully raises funds from new sources rather than poaching funders from existing causes is often notable by its absence in the Jewish world during times of crisis. While evidence-based policymaking does take place in Jewish communities, it is by no means the dominant paradigm.

Jewish organising is often a way of scratching an itch, caused by any number of ticks. Sometimes that tick reminds us that, if things aren't going our way, it's because existing Jewish organisations aren't doing their jobs properly. Since 2000 and the outbreak of the second intifada, an engrained assumption has taken hold among some Jewish leaders, funders and activists that if Israel is being criticised or delegitimised, the reason must be that 'we' are not doing a good enough job in making Israel's case. That belief in the power of *hasbara* ('explanation'), as it is known, has birthed many new organisations and projects. Yet the complaint remains and the proposed solution remains too. Pro-Palestinian activists often ascribe enormous power to the sinister practice of *hasbara*; they should try talking to the latest philanthropist who is convinced that their new outfit will, this time, sweep away the old ineffective explanation with an all-conquering new one.

Sometimes the itch is caused by the tick of over-ambition and is scratched by a scourge of poorly directed spending. I experienced this myself when I attended the European Jewish Parliament, held in Disneyland Paris in April 2011. The brainchild of two Ukrainian-Israeli oligarchs, the EJP, as no one ever refers to it, was intended to rival existing pan-European Jewish bodies in representing Jewish concerns to the European Union. I'd been invited a couple of weeks before by a British Jewish educator who had been charged with finding someone – anyone – to participate in a panel. I accepted out of curiosity and was rewarded by a spectacular display of chaotic incompetence and wasteful over-spending. The event itself went by in a haze of lengthily pointless speeches and equally pointless panels, mediated by simultaneous translation. Planeloads of delegates had been flown in on specially chartered jets from the former Soviet Union. Most of us who attended had no idea why we were there. The lavish gala dinner, held inside Disneyland itself, featured more speeches by grandees who also had no idea why they were there. It was followed by a concert by a well-known Israeli rock singer and his band, brought over at vast expense. I walked back through the park to my hotel and was rewarded by the nightly Disney parade, watched only by me.

A few months later, the EJP announced its first elections. Whoever was running it had the genius idea of allowing open nominations, which led to Sacha Baron-Cohen, David Beckham, Stella McCartney and the French antisemitic comedian Dieudonné M'bala M'bala being proposed. The final list of those elected included representatives of such well-known Jewish hotspots as San Marino and Lichtenstein. I'm fairly well-connected in the UK Jewish community and only recognised the names of a couple of the UK representatives. The 'parliament' went on to meet rarely, there were no further elections and its 'impact' was confined to a few press releases. The EJP no longer exists. One of the oligarchs was arrested for corruption in Ukraine and the other is now sanctioned.

The entire exercise was a total waste of time and money. Or was it? In a world of finite resources, there are many Jewish organisations and projects that seem like a total waste of time and money. It's certainly frustrating that there are many worthy Jewish organisations that have to scramble around for funding while others are deluged with cash to no great purpose. But we shouldn't go too far in castigating Jewish communities for their inefficiency and wastefulness. While some organisations or projects may fail to meet their stated goals, that doesn't mean that they don't provide other benefits. Organisations may achieve things indirectly, even when they fail to achieve their official purpose. Even a project as rich in hubris as the EJP achieved something; I bonded with Jews across Europe in our shared incredulity at the bizarre and ridiculous event. Today, when I meet other attendees at Jewish events, we take a minute to marvel at what happened at Disneyland Paris.

This broader, more indulgent perspective on Jewish organisation can help us understand Jewish doing as something that goes way beyond the purely instrumental. It can even help us appreciate that the apparent futility of some Jewish activities conceals something purposeful. Our 'failures' may be anything but.

Organising our extermination

The *Judenräte*, the Nazi-era Jewish councils that I discussed in Chapter Four, are sometimes remembered as an unforgiveable organisational failure. They did not stop the Holocaust and in some cases they made the process easier for the Nazis to carry out. In the post-war period, the *Judenräte* were often judged harshly, their actions viewed as unforgivable collusion by, for example, Hannah Arendt.

The publication of Isaiah Trunk's history of the *Judenräte* in 1972, helped enable a more measured approach to this painful part of Jewish history.[11] Trunk certainly drew attention to endemic corruption, horrific abuse of power and even at times a degree of enthusiasm with which ghetto police and *Judenräte* officials assisted the Nazis. He also showed the degree of violence with which the Nazis forced existing Jewish leaders to join the councils, as well as the bullying and threats that they suffered to ensure they complied with orders. Yet Jewish 'collusion' was more complicated than it first seems. What began with compulsion often ended up as sophisticated efforts to maximise the chances of Jewish survival. Within a short time, elaborate official bureaucracies had been built in the larger ghettos, working alongside (and sometimes in conflict with) existing Jewish organisations. For example, the 'purveyance agency' in the Warsaw ghetto had 601 distribution points for food and 273 for soap. The 'coal division' had 834 workers and the kitchen division 2,500, based at 130 public kitchens.

It's too simplistic to say that all this activity was for naught, that Warsaw's purveyance agency was worthless as it couldn't prevent mass starvation by supplying one bowl of soup a day. As Trunk suggests, the level of organisation may have been more effective than the Nazis had planned for:

> Urged on by their vitality, traditional ingenuity and skills, and driven by their natural will to live, Jews tried in many ghettos to adjust themselves to the anomalous bitter conditions of their lives. The Jewish reaction to relentless oppression was a complete surprise to the Germans, who had rather expected that simple economic restrictions, continuous hunger, epidemics, and hard labor under impossible conditions would suffice to bring about the morbid results they desired. Can it have been that their disappointment at the – in their view – insufficient results of slow death policies played a role in their decision to turn to mass murder?[12]

The *Judenräte* provide some of the most striking examples of how Jews respond to crisis through organising. Viewed that way, we can maybe empathise better with those Jews who took up roles in a Nazi-created administration. Bureaucracy can feel as solid as bricks and mortar. I look at the labyrinthine institutional machinery of the UK Jewish community, within which I am a cog, and it seems like an impregnable fortress.

Might a Warsaw ghetto bureaucrat toiling in a busy office not be tempted to think that this reality – its paperclips, its reams of paper, its dull meetings – cannot simply be swept away? In her study of prisoner society in the Theresienstadt ghetto, Anna Hájková emphasises how the Jewish bureaucracy allowed at least some inmates a sense of control over their destiny:

> The continuity of bureaucracy could express a sense of order in the horrible new conditions and was hence a means of control. When Jewish functionaries redefined Terezín as a Jewish settlement, they intended to make something good out of something bad; administrative structure was a way to assert control, indeed, to redefine the social space in their own terms. The argument of self-organizing as a form of agency holds true for other ghettos and camps as well, as these often also had a complex system of departments. It is telling, though, that Theresienstadt, which never became a labor ghetto, had by far the most complex organization. The functionaries could not determine everything in the ghetto, but bureaucracy, paperwork, and a formal tone were ways to express agency. And so Theresienstadt became the most organized ghetto of the Holocaust.[13]

There is a long tradition of damning modern bureaucracy as oppressive, impersonal and alienating, the site of absurdity and stupidity. Scholars such as David Graeber, Max Weber and Michel Foucault have shown how the structures that humans build in the modern world take on a life of their own, entrenching systems of domination, imprisoning and infantilising us.[14] There is a related strain of thinking, by Jewish writers such as Zygmunt Bauman, that sees the Holocaust as the brutal apotheosis of modern processes of industrialisation and bureaucratisation.[15]

What this literature can miss, however, is the ways in which bureaucratic rationality can not only provide comfort, but can also help us retain meaning, hope and community in dark times. More than that, bureaucracy can help us *resist*.

Another, even more remarkable feat of ghettoised institution-building achieved at least some of its aims. The 'Ringelbaum Archive' was assembled over the life of the Warsaw ghetto, until its liquidation in the first few months of 1943. The eponymous Emanuel Ringelbaum, a Polish-Jewish historian associated with the left-wing of the Zionist movement, was, even before the war, passionately committed to the work of writing everyday Jewish life back into history. In the Warsaw ghetto, Ringelbaum assembled a secret collective of historians, academics, writers, political activists and others, known under the codename of *Oyneg Shabbos* ('Sabbath Joy'). Working mostly apart from the *Judenrät*, and sometimes in conflict with it, *Oyneg Shabbos* eventually became part of the Jewish resistance movement that grew rapidly from the summer of 1942, when mass deportations started to the extermination camp at Treblinka. The same resistance launched the armed uprising against the Germans in January 1943.[16]

The resistance that Ringelbaum and the *Oyneg Shabbos* practised was a comprehensive attempt to document life in the ghetto, including not just its barbarities, its epidemics and starvation, but also the multiple ways in which Jews and Jewish organisations attempted to find ways to make everyday life liveable. It was an archive of 'everything', as the historian Samuel Kassow recounts:

> The Oyneg Shabes Archive collected both texts and artifacts: the underground press, documents, drawings, candy wrappers, tram tickets, ration cards, theater posters, invitations

to concerts and lectures. It took copies of the convoluted doorbell codes for apartments housing dozens of tenants. There were restaurant menus advertising roast goose and fine wines, and a terse account of a starving mother who had eaten her dead child. Carefully filed away were hundreds of postcards from Jews in the provinces about to be deported to an 'unknown destination.' The Oyneg Shabes preserved the poetry of Władysław Szlengel, Yitzhak Katzenelson, Kalman Lis, and Joseph Kirman. It preserved the entire script of a popular ghetto comedy, 'Love Looks for an Apartment,' and long essays on the ghetto theaters and cafes.[17]

Part of the rationale of the project was to bear witness, particularly once news of the extermination camps filtered into the ghetto and there was no longer doubt as to its ultimate fate. Amazingly, Ringelbaum and the collective succeeded. There was a detailed plan to hide the archive once the uprising began, and it was buried in three milk cans and a number of metal boxes in three different locations within the ghetto. Two of the milk cans were located by survivors after the war; the third has not yet been found. The Ringelbaum Archive remains an unparalleled historical resource and a deeply moving memorial to those who assembled it.

The archive is the product of an extraordinary amount of mundane work. The milk cans were not only filled with cries of pain and anguish. They were filled also, in fact primarily, with documents and ephemera that were not only sober in tone, but also only existed due to bureaucratic labour. It wasn't just the *Judenrät* that pushed paper in the Warsaw Ghetto; *Oyneg Shabbos* did too. This tells us something important about nebulous terms like 'memory', 'bearing witness' and 'resistance';

they can be material practices, created through organising, assembling, collating and – above all – doing. However much Ringelbaum and his associates were living through a nightmare, their days were filled with a myriad of administrative activities. That activity meant that they did not simply feel, they did.

Why Jews organise

It's easy to be awed by Jewish organisational feats such as the Ringelbaum Archive, and it's easy to be impressed with the depth and breadth of the Jewish organisational archipelago today. It's very tempting to conclude that we are very good at this stuff. But I must resist the temptation to posit a Jewish 'genius' for organisation.

Other peoples have also demonstrated extraordinary organisational ability. In Nazi-occupied Poland, Jews certainly reacted to their predicament with extraordinary feats of organisation, but non-Jewish Poles did too. The various underground Polish resistance movements showed extraordinary organisational ability. Aside from a formidable intelligence operation that, among other things, smuggled the first reports of mass exterminations to the Western allies, the Home Army (*Armia Krajowa*), formed in 1942, grew to several hundred-thousand strong against terrible odds. They managed to conduct innumerable sabotage operations and frontal attacks on the occupiers, including the ultimately doomed Warsaw uprising in August 1944. Resistance, Jewish, Polish or otherwise, is not simply a cry of pain; it is most effective when disciplined and bureaucratic.

The Jewish turn to organisation as a source of resilience, hope and comfort in dark times is a trait founded on our propensity to organise in ordinary times. The week that I began work on this chapter, I attended the funeral and *shiva* prayers of the mother of my oldest friend. It was a sad occasion, but it was also a comfortably familiar occasion. I had been to his grandparents' funerals and he had been to mine. My parents and their friends had been there for each other when their parents died, now we were doing the same. I'd been to the cemetery many times before and I had been to *shivas* on countless occasions. All of this took organisation that just seemed to happen. Unofficially, several of our mutual friends took the lead in passing the word around, and soon 'everyone' knew and those of us who could arrange their diaries turned up at the cemetery for the burial.

All of this informal organisation took place alongside the more formal arrangements, guided by the rabbi and synagogue administration. They too were working to a deadline, as Jewish funerals are ideally conducted within 24 hours; although in this case the funeral occurred within 72 hours, some of the preparations were likely completed before that. Before burial the body was washed and prepared by what is known as the *Chevra Kadisha* (the 'holy society'). Mourners' chairs were delivered to the shiva house, the rabbi discussed the service with the mourners, arrangements were made to ensure that my friend's brother (who has learning disabilities) was appropriately supported by the staff of the Jewish group home where he lives. I know that, when it's my turn to mourn or be mourned, everything will fall into place in the same way. It's as though we have been trained for this all our lives.

That 'training' also means that Jews have no fear of starting new Jewish organisations or volunteering for one or many of the myriad existing ones. It is very difficult to find exact numbers, but in the UK – a community of around 300,000 people – a study published in 2019 found there to be about 2,500 Jewish charities in the country.[18] This is around 1.5 per cent of all charities in the UK, for a Jewish population that is 0.5 per cent of the overall population. In addition, there are an uncountable number of Jewish organisations that do not have charitable status, such as some schools, many synagogues, political groups and (often forgotten in discussions of Jewish organisation) businesses that cater to the Jewish population. It's very hard to compare the UK figures to other countries, but the USA, for example, boasts 146 Jewish Federations, most of which support dozens of other organisations. Then there are the synagogues: over 845 Reform ones in the USA, and over 400 of all denominations in the UK.

It would be tedious to run through all the different categories of Jewish organisation. Suffice it to say that they go far beyond catering to religious needs. You can not only 'live' in Jewish organisations from the cradle to the grave – kindergartens to nursing homes – you can also pursue whatever interest that takes your fancy, whether that is in Jewish golf clubs, Jewish hiking groups or Jewish political organisations. While those who see themselves as marginalised by the 'mainstream' Jewish community may complain about their exclusion, the response to this is often to set up a new organisation. The Jewish anti-Zionist left has, in the last few years, developed a substantial network of organisations across the world.

Not only does Jewish organisation require fund-raising, with all the elaborate infrastructure this entails, it also requires people. Those 2,500 Jewish charities in the UK all have to have trustees, lay chairs and, often, professional staff members. Jewish organisations suck in people and they suck in their time. Jewish life is often committee life. I grew up in a household where it was commonplace for one or other parent to rush out after dinner to one committee meeting or another.

My own kids have grown up in a similar household, my wife and I attending countless meetings as Jewish professionals and as volunteers.

What Jews definitely don't organise

This, then, is what supports the supposedly extraordinary Jewish people: A mass of diarising, cajoling, filing, persuading, contacting, accounting, archiving, counting, listing and every other dull gerund you can imagine. Emoting, memorialising, mourning, worrying … all these vivid emotions may be what you see from the outside, and what we Jews sometimes encourage non-Jews to see; but these things are often felt through doing. Behind every Jewish feeling, value or concept there is a Jew pushing paper.

Suspicion at Jewish organisation is a common theme in modern antisemitism. The dense networks that connect Jews to each other, the plurality of Jewish institutions, provide sinister evidence of a global Jewish conspiracy. Like most conspiracy theories, antisemitic myths assume that Jewish organisation is seamless, hyper-efficient, almost telepathic. No people is capable of that and, while I don't think that Jews are any less efficient than anyone else, we certainly have a track record of incompetence and stupidity that can rival any other people's.

In fact, antisemitic views of Jewish organisation may see our sinister genius at work in precisely those areas where we are least competent. One telling example of this was a PowerPoint slide used in a lecture by the British sociologist David Miller. Miller was sacked by Bristol University in 2021 amid bitter controversy over repeated allegations of antisemitism from Jewish students.[19] The slide, a major part of the case against him, purported to show the structure of the Zionist network in Britain. That network encompassed many different Jewish and pro-Israel organisations as well as prominent Jewish leaders and philanthropists. Miller argued that this network was deeply embedded in British social and political life and that what appeared to be a complex structure was evidence of a single subversive power.

In fact, the diagram – or any other attempt to map pro-Israel networks in the UK, US or elsewhere – was evidence of rivalry, grudges, competition, the narcissism of minor differences and endemic inefficiency. The power ascribed to Zionism and the 'Israel lobby' is not always a fantasy – Israel does have many influential advocates around the world – but the evidence that is sometimes presented for its sinister nature is usually evidence of the opposite.

If a global Jewish conspiracy existed, a rival global Jewish conspiracy would undoubtedly be set up. The two conspiracies would compete until they merged, with, naturally, one party to the deal effectively taking over the other. Despite multiple fundraising appeals, the conspiracy would eventually peter out. A few years later a new and similarly ineffective conspiracy would be set up.

Once again, pointing to the existence of Jewish mediocrity and incompetence can be a subversive act, undermining philosemitic and antisemitic narratives alike. It really shouldn't be so shocking to reveal to the world that our desire to organise does not necessarily result in mightily efficient organisations. Organising is difficult and bureaucracy can make idiots of any of us.

What may well be more distinctive, though, is the amount of hope that Jews invest in Jewish organisation. The Jewish tendency to organise as a response to bad things happening is so widespread and so historically persistent that it is hard not to see it as one of our most distinctive traits. To have hope in organisation requires not just hope that organisations will achieve certain ends, but also something more deeply rooted, an implicit conviction that, even if those ends aren't achieved, the process of organisation will have value as an end in and of itself.

To perpetuate organisations with unclear ends in mind (or none at all), to ignore issues of efficiency and competence, is not a sign of a Jewish stupidity. Rather, it stems from a highly distinctive Jewish tendency towards privileging form over content, doing over being, intrinsic value over instrumental value. To understand how that privileging works, you only need to visit a synagogue ...

Chapter Seven
What's the point of it all?

The reason why I Jew

What was the purpose of the Jewish struggle to survive in an often hostile world for millennia? Why are we still being, doing, organising and administrating?

The answer is supper quizzes.

Or at least that's the case in the UK.

The synagogue supper quiz is one of the main events in the ritual calendar. On one evening a year, members gather to eat fish and chips (or sometimes falafel) and then each table competes for the title of ... well, there is rarely an actual title involved. The questions are set by a trivia-minded member of the community or outsourced to Jewish quiz-obsessives that tour the supper-quiz circuit. The teams confer after each question and write the answers on a sheet that is sent to be 'marked' by the assistants to the quizmaster or mistress. Things can get a bit competitive but it's all good, clean fun.

Synagogue supper quizzes are more or less unknown outside the UK. The quiz night is a popular British leisure time activity, usually held in pubs. Synagogue supper quizzes have their own idiosyncrasies, though. There's little drinking involved, the food is of much greater importance (regular pub quizzes are, understandably enough, designed to sell drinks, although one pub quiz I used to attend did serve free chips). In other respects, the synagogue supper quiz wears its Jewishness lightly. There may or may not be a question round on a Jewish theme, and most rounds aren't that different from what you'd find in pubs.

So much of synagogue life is spent organising and participating in such 'peripheral' activities. I asked my wife to name a US state at random. She chose Alabama and I then googled 'Alabama synagogue'. The first one to appear in the results was Temple Beth-El in Birmingham.[1] Their events calendar included 'Movie Talk Village' (discussing *A Serious Man*), 'Our Lives as Seen Through Each Other' (no idea), a 'Docent Workshop' (ditto), a walk to 'Enon Ridge and the old Jewish cemetery' and 'Stop The Bleed Training'. The synagogue's men's club were organising a trip to watch Birmingham Barons take on the Pensacola Blue Wahoos (they'd managed to secure a group rate for tickets behind the home plate). All this was, of course, in addition to the daily, Shabbat and festival services, classes for all ages and welfare activities.

Few people, Jewish or otherwise, would treat supper quizzes and trips to watch minor league baseball as the central purpose of synagogue life. But ascertaining the purpose of human institutions is not as simple as one might think. In her classic essay 'Food as an art form' (first delivered as a lecture in 1974), the anthropologist Mary Douglas posed the following thought experiment:

> Imagine a competent young anthropologist arriving on this planet from Mars and setting out to study the culture of the English natives. He would try to attend all their ceremonies. Sooner or later he would start being invited to weddings and there he would be perhaps baffled to make up his mind whether the central focus of the ceremony was the marriage or the cake.[2]

How do we know that the purpose of weddings isn't the cake? The cutting of the cake occurs near the end of the reception – a climactic moment – and is usually accompanied by joy, laughter and merriment. The cake is usually expensive and far more lavish than ordinary cakes. The married couple may save slices of the cake in the freezer for years and photos of them cutting the cake take pride of place on many mantelpieces.

One sign that the cutting of the cake is not the purpose of the wedding is that wedding invitations never invite guests to come to the 'cutting of the cake ceremony'. Yet it may well be the bit of the wedding that some couples and guests enjoy the most and look forward to. It's certainly possible to want to get married in order to have a big party and wear a beautiful dress; it's equally possible for a wedding guest to treat the reception simply as an excuse to drink and be merry. So why is it unreasonable to imagine someone getting married out of a desire to cut a large, multi-layered white cake? And why is it ridiculous to imagine that some synagogue members might see a supper quiz as the principal membership benefit? Certainly, there is a lot of passion and boisterous joviality in a supper quiz – much more than in prayer – so why wouldn't you assume it was the point of the synagogue?

To think of the rituals, institutions and practices of social life in terms of their 'purpose' may feel like the obvious thing to do. In fact, the search for underlying purpose is a more culturally specific activity than it might appear. There is a longstanding fascination within 'Western' philosophy, society and culture in the 'essence' of things, in what lies beneath the surface appearance of life. The ancient Greeks (Plato in particular) wrestled with identifying the essence of beauty and other ideals. Christians wrestled with (and, in the Reformation, fought and died for) the mysterious nature of the eucharist, the ability of mundane bread and wine to change its essence to the body and blood of Christ while retaining the same outward form.

The modern world was forged through 'enlightened' ideas of the exact essence of a nation, a 'race', a deviant or a sex.

An 'essentialist' view of the world is suspicious of the form in which the world appears to us. The way things seem must necessarily conceal a fundamental, motivating purpose. That which cannot be easily assigned in such a way is at best an anachronism and at worst a dangerous impurity. If a synagogue's essential purpose is to gather together Jews in prayer and study, then the supper quiz must either be a ritual that helps to create the conditions for gathering Jews together in prayer, or it is 'just' a bit of harmless fun that uses the synagogue as an excuse, or it is a degradation of the holy purpose of the synagogue.

Jews are certainly capable of thinking in essentialist terms. Indeed, in the Haredi world, a synagogue supper quiz would be seen as a distraction from the purpose of Jewish life, which is dedication to Torah. Jews wrestled with the Greeks too, sometimes antagonistically and sometimes more sympathetically. The medieval philosopher Maimonides sought to boil down Judaism to its essence as a coherent set of beliefs. There is a rich Jewish tradition of looking beyond the surface appearance of things to the mysteries beyond. In reading Torah and other canonical texts, there is an entire system for looking beyond the *p'shat*, the plain meaning, towards deeper meanings. The kabbalistic tradition, Judaism's mystical path, is predicated on a universe that is beyond our daily imaginings.

We Jews are not a purely superficial people. We do sometimes seek depth. But, crucially, Jewish tradition does not denigrate the surface level in which everyday life is led. Over millennia, Judaism has built up a system of law and practice that is all-encompassing, complex and demanding. Ideally, adherence to that system should be suffused with purposeful attention to the divine, known as *kavanah*. In reality, as in any other system, attention is a precious commodity. To live purely in the realm of the holiness that lies beyond each infinitesimal Jewish action may only be possible for a select number of adepts. And how would we know if such a holy character wasn't just faking it?

Actually, that applies more widely: who knows what is going on people's heads? How do we even know if we are doing *kavanah*? What proof is there of our progress towards *deveykut* (cleaving to the divine)? That is a problem common to all religions, but in Judaism it is far easier to ignore it than in some other traditions. Not only is there just so much stuff to do that there is little space for open-ended introspection, Judaism combines a very heavy burden of doing with a very light burden of punishment. There is a Jewish concept of the afterlife; there are rewards and punishment for behaviour in this world that are paid in the next one. This concept is pretty vague, though, and lacks the terrifying imminence found in some forms of Christianity.

All of this means that it is perfectly possible, and maybe normative, to live a Jewish life as a ceaseless flow of doing, a continuous present, free of the burdens of that which is beyond. Jewish doing can be doing for its own sake or for no sake at all.

Reasons to be Jewish
At this point you might be thinking that my argument applies only to traditionally observant Jews who are committed to the system of Jewish law in all its breadth and depth. One might expect that it is only the most observant for whom doing is so overwhelming that it leaves little space for introspection and appreciation of the Godhead. But the situation is more nuanced than that.

Even 'lax' Jewish observance can be taxing. Take the example of the fabled 'twice a year' Jew, one who only attends synagogue on Rosh Hashanah and Yom Kippur. Not only is such a Jew committed enough to lavish extortionate membership fees on an organisation they barely engage with, but these festivals also require considerable effort to even nominally celebrate them. It is perfectly common for a Jew to spend Yom Kippur fasting for 25 hours, attending services for around eight hours – and then going on to say that they aren't very religious.

Some strains of progressive Judaism view excessive emphasis on ritual and practice as a barrier to divine contemplation. One of the defining characteristics of most progressive synagogues is that the liturgy is much less voluminous than in orthodox synagogues. In the latter, prayer is conducted at breakneck speed, almost entirely in Hebrew and Aramaic, becoming almost mantra-like in its chanting. Progressive worship is slower and includes the vernacular. That emphasis on clarity can be paradoxically uncomfortable for some of us; it gives us no place to hide from meaning and the divine. In some synagogues and for some progressive thinkers, there's even a whiff of Christianity in treating liturgy 'instrumentally', as a carrier of meaning: content over form.

One common assumption behind attempts to tackle the 'threat' of assimilation has been that there needs to be a reason to be Jewish and that Jews are turned off by a lack of meaningful spiritual content in 'mainstream' Jewish life. Steven Cohen and Arnold Eisen's 2000 book *The Jew Within*, a study of 'moderately affiliated' Jews in the US, found that their respondents often saw Jewishness through the lens of the 'sovereign self' and situated their engagement with Judaism within the narrative of life as a journey, a quest for meaning.[3] At the time, the publication of the book occasioned much hand-wringing by Jewish leaders. Some saw Jews of this kind as irredeemably self-centred, others saw the findings as a call to respond to those frustrated seekers after meaning.

Jews who seek meaning as part of a personal spiritual journey shouldn't necessarily be seen as self-centered, or if they are, it isn't the main problem. For me, the problem is that such seekers often yearn for a 'deeper' reason to do and be Jewish. It is hard to live an everyday Jewish life to its fullest without at least some capacity to do Jewish for the sake of doing Jewish. Of course, one might argue that this kind of everyday Jewishness is not the only legitimate form of Jewishness. Spiritual seekers have been responsible for some of the most dramatic and important innovations in the history of Judaism. But we can actually make a sturdy theological case for a Jewish practice that emphasises doing and sees introspection and spiritual seeking as an optional extra.

The Jewish God is a distant God, at least these days. While the Jewish God does care for its creation and has intervened and spoken to its people, it is ultimately alien to us. As God told Moses, humans cannot see God directly and live. God has a form that is beyond the material. Even God's name is too holy to be uttered; only the high priest at the Temple, when it still stood, knew it and could utter it and then only in private. That distance from the divine is precisely what allows humans to exercise agency. There is a famous Talmudic story in which God intervenes in a bitter dispute about whether a particular kind of oven can be ritually pure. The ancient rabbis exerted pressure over Rabbi Eleazer, who dissented from the consensus. When a voice from heaven intervenes on Rabbi Eleazer's side, Rabbi Joshua retorts that 'The Torah is not in heaven'. As proof, he points to the words of Deuteronomy chapter 30:12–14:

It is not in the heavens, that you should say, 'Who among us can go up to the heavens and get it for us and impart it to us, that we may observe it?' Neither is it beyond the sea, that you should say, 'Who among us can cross to the other side of the sea and get it for us and impart it to us, that we may observe it?' No, the thing is very close to you, in your mouth and in your heart, to observe it.[4]

Jewish observance and practice, while taxing, is rooted in the capacities that humans have. That includes the capacity to interpret the divine will within everyday life in ways that are practical and human-centred.

One of the twentieth century's most unique Jewish voices, Yeshayahu Leibowitz, was once asked why the chicken crossed the road. His answer was as follows:

Stupid question. We simply follow the *halacha* [system of law]. The chicken crosses the road. That's it.[5]

Leibowitz, a professor at Hebrew University in Jerusalem who died in 1994, is best known these days for his incendiary comments that the Israeli occupation forces acted as 'Judeo-Nazis'. That gets him a lot of love these days in anti-Zionist circles but, as a theologian, his view of Jewish law was anything but self-righteous. Leibowitz's God is so transcendent and impersonal, and so opaque in its purpose, that there is no knowing why we should obey God's law. To live as a Jew who keeps the law – as Leibowitz, an orthodox Jew, did – is not to hope for divine favour in this world or the next, nor is there necessarily even an ethical dimension to it. We should just do. That's it. His view of prayer denigrates the spontaneous prayer of individual Jews. In fact, he argues that, as with any *mitzvah*, prayer only has religious value when one is obligated to perform it, regardless of one's actual needs:

The grandeur and power of prayer, prayer that is mandatory and fixed by Halakhah [Jewish law], lie precisely in setting aside all of man's interests and motives out of awareness of man's position before God, a position which is always the same regardless of any personal circumstances. Man relinquishes his own will in the recognition of the duty of worship. The same set of eighteen benedictions is required of the bridegroom as of the widower returning from his wife's funeral. The same series of psalms is recited by one enjoying the world and one whose world has collapsed. The identical supplications are required of those who feel the need for them and those who do not.[6]

Superficially, Leibowitz's theology is so austere that it would repel many Jews. At the same time, this 'just do it' rationale for Jewish practice does describe how, in effect, Jewish lives are often lived. In the UK, for example, whereas Christian practice is declining at a far greater rate than belief in the divine ('believing without belonging'), for Jews it's the opposite, as 2024 figures from the Institute for Jewish Policy Research demonstrate:

If only a third of Jews have faith in God, as described in the Bible, where does that leave Judaism? Is it inevitably on the same downward path as Christianity? Not necessarily. A key indicator of the decline of organised religion in Britain is 'bums-on-pews' – i.e. that only people who believe in God are likely to attend church. Even if that is true, it doesn't seem to apply to Jews. In the Jewish case, according to the survey's data, more than half (56%) of paid-up synagogue members do not believe in God, and nearly two in five Jewish *atheists* belong to a synagogue. Moreover, irrespective of whether they belong to a synagogue or not, two out of three (65%) Jews who don't believe in God attend synagogue at least on the High Holy Days of Rosh Hashana and Yom Kippur. Jews, it seems, are pretty comfortable belonging without believing.[7]

The Jewish world is highly fragmented. What unity there is lies in the propensity to do. Jews do the same things for very different reasons. Jewish life makes little sense if you don't acknowledge that belief and practice do not always align. The results are often bizarre, sometimes hilarious, and that is something Jews should celebrate.

Happy hypocrites

One of my favourite moments at any British Jewish Bar/Bat Mitzvah or wedding is when the dancing starts and the floor turns into a giant mosh pit, everyone screaming out the following words:

Mashiach, mashiach, mashiach!
Oy yoi yoi yoi yoi yoi
Mashiach, mashiach, mashiach!
Oy yoi yoi yoi yoi yoi

The lyrics of the verse leave you in no doubt what the song is about, if you can understand the Hebrew, at least. Here they are in English:

I believe, I believe
With perfect faith
In the coming of Mashiach

The words are taken from one of Maimonides' thirteen principles of faith:

> I believe with perfect faith in the coming of mashiach, and
> though he may tarry, still I await him every day

Mashiach is the messiah, a scion of the dynasty of King David
who will come at some point to redeem the Jewish people and
through them the world. I don't believe with perfect faith in
the coming of mashiach. Nor do most of the Jews I associate
with, although some might profess a belief in a less-literal kind
of 'messianic age'. The reason why everyone I know adores
the song is simple: It's an absolute banger. I once attended a
wedding of a progressive rabbinic student and witnessed the
wonderful site of a gaggle of other progressive rabbis and rabbinic students singing and dancing along passionately (although
one of them tried to change the messiah's gender to the feminine – *mashicha*). I have no idea what Mordechai ben David,
the Hasidic singer who wrote the song, would think about this
profession of faith being professed by the faithless – and with
mixed dancing too! – but great music has a life of its own.

There is something gloriously blasphemous in profess-
ing faith you don't have because you like a particular tune.
Outside of the strictest orthodox communities, there are endless ways of practising Jewishly through a joyfully incoherent
mess of contradiction, transgression and affirmation. My wife,
who grew up in Houston, remembers something called 'Texas
kosher': keeping kosher but eating shellfish. She recalls her
grandmother, who kept a strictly kosher home, eating shrimp
cocktail in the garage. In the UK most members of the main
orthodox denomination do not adhere completely to orthodox
practice; it's common to park around the corner from the synagogue on Shabbat and then walk the rest of the way, in order to
not be seen to transgress commandments against using powered
devices on the Sabbath.

When I was young, I thought this kind of Jewish practice hypocritical. Indeed, the progressive Jewish tradition in which I was raised has often seen itself as a Judaism that aligns with its members' values and beliefs. Over time I came to question whether hypocrisy is necessarily such a terrible thing. One interviewee in a research project I worked on, a committed member of an orthodox synagogue who was fine with driving on Shabbat, told me that she and her family were 'happy hypocrites'.[8] And why shouldn't they be happy?

I am not going to go as far as saying it's easy to be a practising Jew and a confirmed atheist. What *is* easy is to simply not care very much whether God exists or not. In fact, I have become suspicious of those times when belief and doing coincide. In my synagogue, the sight I fear most is a fellow worshipper beatifically smiling in the light of the divine. Fortunately, it doesn't happen that much. If Jews started publicly displaying belief in this way, we'd never be able to keep the show on the road. It is only through emphasising what we do, rather than what we think, that we can maintain community and avoid schisms even worse than the ones we have already suffered.

Of course, there are times when Jewish resistance to meaning curdles into something regressive. I found one extraordinary example of this in an interview I conducted as part of the same research project in which I met the happy hypocrite. It was with a middle-aged man in Glasgow who was a member of an orthodox synagogue but was not orthodox practising himself. Nonetheless, he had strong views about what was Jewishly permissible and what was not. I asked him whether his daughter had a *bat chayil*, a ceremony for girls held in some orthodox synagogues where girls are not permitted to have a *bat mitzvah*:

Q: Did your daughter have a bat chayil?

A: No, she did not. I felt very unhappy about that.

Q: Why didn't she have?

A: Because I was disapproving of bat chayil, because I felt that in my time there was no such thing as a bat chayil or, if there was, it was unheard of. I felt that a bat chayil was something that Lubavitch [the strictly orthodox denomination the rabbi was part of] had set up to satisfy the female Jewish population and I felt that my daughter wanted a bat chayil for the wrong reasons and not the right reasons.

Q: Was she unhappy about it?

A: She was very unhappy about it, yes.

This Jewish man was so committed to the 'proper' doing of Jewish life that even a far more Jewishly observant and knowledgeable rabbi was not 'qualified' to decide what was appropriate. None of this difference of opinion was theologically based. Everyday Jewishness can override meaning itself and curdle into stubborn prejudice.

Doing for the sake of doing

Even though 'meaningless' Judaism can have negative effects, I doubt that it would be possible to keep many synagogues going without at least some capacity in their members and volunteers to find satisfaction in doing for the sake of doing. I saw that in my own upbringing. My father chaired the 'ritual committee' for many years. Most synagogues have a committee like this to organise the nuts and bolts of services. It's the sort of work that, when successful, no one notices, and God help you if you aren't successful; certainly no one thanks you for doing it. The committee's most important task was arranging services for Rosh Hashanah and Yom Kippur, when the congregation swelled to many times its usual size. This was particularly challenging in my synagogue, as the building we had was many times too small for this expanded congregation. My father spent thankless days searching for buildings that could accommodate us, such as schools and sports halls; none of them were particularly satisfactory, all of them needing to be transformed in some way to be at least slightly spiritual. The real kick in the teeth was on Yom Kippur when, at the end of a 25-hour fast, most of the congregation rushed to get home and my dad and a small group of other suckers, including myself, had to get all the ritual accoutrements, books and so forth, into the van that one of our members drove. I remember desperately stuffing chollah into my mouth before carrying Torah scrolls out of the building on shaky legs.

There can be deep satisfaction in this work, however thankless. I was proud of my dad then, as now, and I think he felt it was worthwhile. So unnoticed and unappreciated is this kind of work that I don't think it's possible to do it year after year without some kind of intrinsic reward. And I felt a bit of that too. There was a kind of enjoyment in being part of the engine room that propelled our congregation forward, almost a superiority in waiting longer to break the Yom Kippur fast than most of my fellow members.

Perhaps one of the reasons why Jewish doing for the sake of doing isn't as acknowledged as it should be, is that it raises the possibility that what Jews do is what others do too. My dad and I once had to take down the set for a musical that my friends and I put on in a village hall. It really didn't feel that different from packing up after Yom Kippur. Carrying a box to a van is not a uniquely Jewish experience.

You can often find something universal in even the most apparently insular Jewish practices. I once stumbled across a YouTube video from 2010 of Rabbi Yosef Shalom Elyashiv studying in his apartment.[9] Elyashiv, who died in 2012 aged 102, was the pre-eminent authority on Jewish law in the so-called 'Lithuanian' stream of strictly orthodox Jewry, which prides itself on its austere commitment to Torah study above all things. The video, which first tours Elyashiv's modest book-lined apartment, goes on to look over his shoulder as he is transfixed in poring over a page of Talmud. He chants key passages, rocking back and forth with the intensity of his learning. The title of the video proclaims that Rabbi Eliyashiv is *shtaigging*, a Yiddish term for spiritual ascent through learning.

To me, it looked like he was in geek heaven.

The Talmud is so full of detail, obscurity and complexity that, if you are a particular kind of person, you can lose yourself in it and never come out. That love of minutiae – the more gnomic the better – is common to many scholarly fields, but also to hobby and fan cultures. It's no accident that many of the rabbis I know – including the one I am married to – are sci-fi geeks. While I am pretty sure Rabbi Eliyashiv never watched *Star Trek*, he didn't need to; he had the good fortune to be born into a culture where the Torah geek is venerated to the extent that he had little need to do anything other than study and rule on complex problems of Jewish law.

The mechanics of doing can transcend the superficial purpose of what one does, at least to a degree. That transcendence may be one of the things that makes Jewish doing so distinctive. The overwhelming amount of stuff that Jews do creates the ideal conditions for the decoupling of the act and its notional purpose. It's easy to do without asking why or for what purpose. While that may make Jews sound like automatons, in fact not asking why ensures that Jewish life can be open to a vast range of experiences that Jews can lose themselves in. There is something for everyone. While Jews who are not orthodox may often do 'less', they remain within the welcoming embrace of 'meaningless' Jewish doing.

This meaninglessness is not something we Jews talk about very much; when we do, it is usually to decry it. If Rabbi Eliyashiv came back to life and read the previous paragraphs he would undoubtedly defend the sanctity of his *shtaigging*. Official representatives of the main Jewish denominations insist on the meaning and purpose of their way of doing Jewish. We live within a world where meaninglessness is not seen as a good thing and doing for the sake of doing seems, well, pointless.

Reasons to fight antisemitism

Acknowledging the propensity of Jews to do for the sake of doing can be particularly difficult when it comes to fighting antisemitism. Here, there are definite advantages to positioning ourselves primarily as Jews who feel, rather than Jews who do.

In most countries today, synagogues and some other Jewish buildings have surveillance cameras and other defensive measures. In places where there have been fatal terrorist attacks on Jewish targets, these defensive measures can lead to buildings looking like fortresses. A few years ago I attended a conference held on the premises of the Copenhagen Jewish school. The campus was surrounded by high walls, and to get in, visitors had to pass through bomb-proof gates and armed security. That was all understandable given that in February 2015, a Jewish security guard protecting a bat mitzvah celebration in the synagogue in the centre of Copenhagen was shot and killed by a terrorist seeking to avenge the Danish publication of a cartoon of Muhammad. Security in Jewish Copenhagen is far more visible than it once was.

In the UK, we have yet to see a fatal terrorist attack on a Jewish building, although graffiti, vandalism and insults certainly do happen. We do have a complex security infrastructure, although in most locations it falls short of the fortress approach. In fact, that infrastructure, as it has developed in the last few decades, is founded on one of the great rituals of British Jewish life – the security rota. When I was growing up, my parents took their turn to be 'on security'. That meant standing in front of the synagogue. That's it. The logic was that 'opportunistic' attacks are less likely if a building has someone clearly standing outside it. Over the years, security in the British Jewish community has become more sophisticated. When I started to take my own turn on the security rota at a different synagogue, I was given a walkie-talkie. The other volunteers and I were coordinated by a volunteer trained by the Community Security Trust (CST). At most big Jewish events in the UK you will see CST volunteers, looking serious, walkie-talkie earpiece in one ear and wearing stab-proof vests.

The existence of this security infrastructure sometimes shocks non-Jews. Jewish leaders are not above publicly lamenting the need for it. Politicians are always ready to get an easy win by dropping a few million pounds into synagogue security. Conversely, the CST is often the target of scorn from Jewish and non-Jewish critics for exaggerating the risks Jews actually face.

What these perspectives do not take into account is that volunteering for security duty at one's synagogue or doing more serious training with the CST is quite satisfying, even enjoyable. Perhaps for some it endows an inflated sense of self-importance, but where's the harm in that? In any case, to be a security volunteer is a way of contributing to and finding pleasure in community. For some Jews it's the main thing they do Jewishly. I have a colleague who is a member of a synagogue he never sets foot in but loves to do security on Rosh Hashanah and Yom Kippur; a sociable character, he knows that outside the building is the place to be, to greet friends and acquaintances old or new.

Viewed this way, volunteering for security is less fear of antisemitism incarnate, more like finding satisfaction in doing an important job with like-minded people. Volunteering – of any kind – allows us to be and do something different than in one's regular life. It can be a glimpse of another existence. For example, one of the events that the CST provides security for is the Limmud conference, held over the Christmas period every year. One year, when Limmud was held on a large university campus, my wife and I had to leave earlier than planned. I collected our car and drove round to collect her from one of the more isolated buildings. It was dark, cold and rainy. As I waited in my nice warm car I was surprised by a knock on the window. It was a CST volunteer, a slightly built woman in her early twenties, checking who I was and what I was doing there.

At the time I found this irritating and intrusive. What if I wasn't Jewish and had a reason to be there? I suppose some might see this as a disgraceful reminder of how Jews are so threatened that young women have to put themselves in jeopardy to protect us, or from the opposite perspective a damning example of how the community has brainwashed its young to the point that they risk their own safety out of illusory fears. What I have eventually come to realise is that any community that can enable a young woman to spend her holiday period conducting solitary patrols around a dark university campus in the middle of an English winter must have something going for it. The antisemitism is only half the point; it's the culture of doing things with other Jews that matters most.

The problem the CST has is that it will have trouble attracting funding and other kinds of support if it makes too much of the fact that aside from protecting the UK Jewish community from antisemitism, it is also a social club and a way of enabling Jews to dip into and out of a different kind of life. That's the dilemma that Jews have when it comes to acknowledging who we are; in representing ourselves to the wider public and to other Jews, it's risky to mention that the ostensible purpose of Jewish organisations may not be the whole story. The trouble is that failing to mention it also carries its own risks. When it comes to public image, we don't want to be seen as a community of happy hypocrites.

As a teenager, I experienced the consequences of failing to understand the purpose of a particular Jewish practice. When I was fifteen years old I attended a summer camp in the Netherlands, run by the UK branch of the Zionist youth movement Habonim, which developed out of the socialist-Zionist tradition. My parents, who wanted me to socialise with other Jews during the summer holiday, persuaded me to attend Habonim as I was left-wing too. And yes, the ideology of the youth movement was left-wing and I did enjoy the educational activities. The problem was that the ideological stance of Habonim, while it was certainly proclaimed at every opportunity, was utterly irrelevant to the real business of the camp: frenzied socialising and coupling. Habonim's culture of extrovert cockiness that stoked the social whirl (Sacha Baron-Cohen, Habonim's most famous alumnus, exemplifies this culture) was hugely intimidating. I spent most of that holiday miserable and bewildered.

By the next summer, I had learned my lesson: Never again would I treat the stated purpose of Jewish youth activities as their actual purpose. I refused to join one of the key rites of passage in British Jewry, the post-sixteen month-long tour of Israel. Hugely popular then and now, a variety of different youth movements run these tours, but I wasn't going to take the risk of taking their various ideologies seriously. I knew that Israel tour was about spending a month getting on and off a coach amid endless flirtation and gossip. I didn't trust that any of the youth movements would have a culture in which I could find my place. If there had been such a culture, I wouldn't have cared what the youth movement's ideology consisted of. At that point I'd have helped settle the West Bank if there was a chance that I could hook up with someone.

Of course, Jewish leaders are not idiots; they know that Israel tours and summer camps are crucibles in which young Jews couple, de-couple and bond. In fact, in the case of Israel tours for 20- and 30-somethings, forming Jewish couples and preventing intermarriage is part of the whole strategy. Diaspora and Israeli Jewish organisations have invested heavily in tours for teenagers and young adults, because they 'work'. Yet there's still a gap between the lofty visions of profound engagement with Israel and Judaism, and the earthy reality. Ironically, those who run and fund these activities may be on the same page as pro-Palestinian activists and Jewish anti-Zionists who see Zionist youth movements and Israel tours as brainwashing. In reality, if they do create a stronger bond with Israel, it's also because Israel becomes the backdrop to peak experiences. There isn't any need to push a party line on participants; frankly, if your first kiss took place during a tour of Düsseldorf or Des Moines, you'd likely have warm, fuzzy feelings about those places.

There's nothing particularly unusual about activities and organisations for whom there is both an official an unofficial purpose. The Jewish way of doing is unusual only in its extent. The problem is that Jewish reluctance to publicly acknowledge the tendency of Jews to do for the sake of doing makes it a kind of private secret, to be discussed only among Jews with the microphone off. That secrecy creates a kind of banal doppelganger of the secretive Jew that exists in the antisemitic imagination. It leads us to represent Jewish life in distorted ways. As I will show in the next chapter, that distortion can become dangerous when Jews enter the realm of public politics.

Chapter Eight

The great Chanukah swindle

Come bathe in our light

Just after the end of Chanukah 2024, the UK Reform Movement sent out an email to its members.[1] The headline read 'Historic Chanukah lightings show growth of Progressive Judaism'. Why 'historic'? Only a few months before, the Reform Movement had agreed to a merger with the Liberal Movement, and the anomalous existence of two similar movements would be replaced with a Progressive Movement. The leaders of the two movements – Rabbi Josh Levy (Reform) and Rabbi Charley Baginsky (Liberal) – were working hard to create a buzz around the merger. Chanukah, therefore, was a big opportunity:

> Progressive Judaism Co-Leads Rabbis Josh Levy and Charley Baginsky were at different Chanukah events every night of the festival. These included celebrations hosted in 10 Downing Street, Speaker's House, Wembley Stadium, the Guildhall, the residence of the American Ambassador and by the Jewish Labour Movement and Standing Together. At the Westminster Hall event – the first to take place in that historic venue – Rabbi Charley was one of those who lit candles, alongside Home Secretary James Cleverly, Labour leader Sir Keir Starmer, Liberal Democrat Leader Sir Ed Davey, event organiser Lord (John) Mann and Chief Rabbi

of United Hebrew Congregations of the Commonwealth
Sir Ephraim Mirvis ... Rabbi Josh lit the candles at events
including the City of London Corporation celebrations in
the historic Livery Hall.

The two rabbis were not the only ones who had a busy
Chanukah. The President of the Board of Deputies attended
some of the same candle lightings, as well as others organised
by the UK Foreign Minister, the Mayor of London and with
senior Labour Party politicians at the home of one of the leaders of London's strictly orthodox Jewish community. Across
London and the UK – actually across the globe – the Chabad-
Lubavitch movement organised public candle lightings at
numerous strategically sited giant *menorot,* as it has done
since the 1970s. Naturally, Chanukah was also celebrated in
the White House.

Chanukah has become Judaism's most visible festival. As well
as public candle-lightings, Chanukah has become part of the
Christmas season in many countries. Although some Jews view
this with ambivalence, there's no doubt that the easy availability
of Chanukah cards, decorations and gift items 'normalises' the
festival. At the very least, the association between Chanukah
and Christmas does encourage a 'See? They are just like us!'
discourse, which may be simplistic but can be helpful in making
Jews less mysterious.

It would be completely reasonable to conclude from the
public visibility of Chanukah that this is our most important
festival. While 'officially', Judaism doesn't rank festivals in
order of importance, Chanukah certainly is one of the festivals
that even Jews who do little else may mark in some way. It is
definitely a festival that can be fun to celebrate; who doesn't like
doughnuts, candles and presents? Yet Chanukah's popularity

and visibility ultimately conceal something. It is not entirely what it appears.

When my wife was teaching *cheder*, she would introduce Chanukah by passing out Bibles and asking her pupils to find the Chanukah story. Of course, they failed. Chanukah does not appear in the Hebrew Bible; the story is found in the first and second books of Maccabees, which were not ultimately included in the biblical canon. The Chanukah story is a story about and for Jews. It is a story of Jews rebelling against Antiochus, a Hellenistic king of the Seleucid Empire, who despoiled the Temple in Jerusalem and enforced worship of the Greek gods. The holiday celebrates the Maccabean Jews who rebelled against Antiochus and rededicated the Temple in around 166 BCE. The lighting of candles over the eight nights of Chanukah follows a later account, recorded in the Talmud, that when the Temple was rededicated, there was only one day's oil for the sacred light, yet this oil miraculously lasted for eight days until more could be found.

While there is no historical evidence for this miracle and the accounts of the story in the books of Maccabees are of uncertain accuracy, Chanukah does recall a bitter dispute both within the Jewish people and with the great powers of the time. The Maccabees stood for unapologetic Jewish particularism, an insular form of practice centred around the performance of Temple rites; a Judaism for Jews. In contrast, the Hellenised world could be for 'everyone', at least in theory. This universalism offered the tempting possibility for Jews and other peoples to become part of the expanding prestige culture of the day. When the Maccabees rebelled, they were also rebelling against Jews who were tempted by Athens over Jerusalem.

That conflict between Athens and Jerusalem has become a key conceptual dichotomies through which many modern intellectuals have come to understand the tensions within Judaism, both in ancient times and today. The Maccabees did not triumph permanently; Judaism has within it both universalist and particularist elements, and disputes over the appropriate balance between the two have flared up repeatedly. Such conflict provides part of the political-religious context in which Jesus intervened, leading eventually to the unabashed universalism of Paul that was to forge a whole new religion. Today that conflict flares up in Israel and the Diaspora, as Jews argue over how far we should be for ourselves alone and how far for universal human values.

Chanukah definitely concerns Jerusalem, not Athens. So it seems an extraordinary irony that Chanukah has become our most outward-facing festival. It's even more extraordinary that it has become a celebration of harmonious multiculturalism and respectful interfaith relations. The Maccabees were not celebrating diversity when they took up arms. When I witness public candle-lighting I always feel a knot of anxiety: What would happen if our non-Jewish guests *found out*?

In fairness, Chanukah isn't just a festival for cheerleading protagonists in a millennia-old rebellion. There are mystical traditions that give the festival greater gravity and make the lights stand for something more than long-life oil; Chanukah is a rich source of spiritual riffing on darkness, light and redemption. Still, you have to work pretty hard to find a general lesson for the world. The UK branch of Chabad-Lubavitch came up with this:

> The Menorah also has **universal significance for all humanity**: The battle of the Jews against the ancient Syrian – Greeks was a battle for belief in one G-d and for the **universal moral values** implicit in that belief.[2]

In other words, by vanquishing Athens, we Jews have ensured that we are all Jerusalem now. Aside from being historically dubious, this attempt only manages to make Chanukah universalist by blowing the particular up to monstrous proportions. This is fairly desperate stuff, and online browsing reveals that there's loads of strained analogy to go round. Take this extract from an article from the website of a Jewish addictions charity:

> The Chanukah candles inspire us to be constantly striving upward, improving as we go. The menorah's candles increase one each night, demonstrating that this kind of growth is a process, one that typically happens in incremental steps. When dealing with addiction, **patience is the key.**[3]

While the article this quote has been taken from is targeted at Jews, it really just uses a Chanukah ritual as a way of reinforcing a message that applies to all addicts, Jews or otherwise. Such clumsy usage reveals a wider phenomenon, a kind of discomfort, particularly among Jews who are not orthodox, with the particularist zealotry of the Chanukah story. Making Chanukah public and universal is one way of assuaging that anxiety.

There is one part of the Chanukah ritual that has always been public, though: The lit menorah is generally placed on a window ledge, a doorway or other place where it can be seen. This is a gesture that can be understood in different ways. It might be from an open-hearted desire to share the light of the festival with Jewish and non-Jewish neighbours. It also might be seen as defiance; as in the famous photograph taken in Germany in 1931 of a lit menorah shining on the windowsill of an apartment that faced a large Nazi flag opposite.[4]

Whatever the public display of lit menorot has meant in different places at different points in history, there are precedents for today's even more public candle-lightings. There are definitely good reasons for 'choosing' Chanukah as our most public festival regardless of the ironies of doing so. The major Jewish festivals aren't easily shared as most mandate Shabbat-style restrictions on labour and the use of cars, machinery and electronic gadgets. This means that, in orthodox contexts, you can't use a PA, be filmed or do a myriad other things that public celebration with non-Jews would entail. Even in non-orthodox circles, some of these prohibitions remain culturally mandated at least. The major festivals can also be too solemn to work as public outreach. A non-Jewish girlfriend once, in all innocence, assumed that Jews dance and party on Rosh Hashanah, the Jewish new year (if only!). In addition, on most of the major festivals there is so much for Jews to do that welcoming guests for public ceremonies would be too much of a burden. Jewish festival prayers go on for hours, to say nothing of ancillary rituals such as studying all night on Shavuot.

Chanukah fits the bill perfectly. There are no prohibitions on work, few mandated rituals and a choice of dates over the eight nights. While Pesach does give Chanukah a run for its money outreach-wise – seders have even been held in the White House – it is ultimately too complex to allow for easy repackaging. Chanukah just *works*. More than that, it fills a desire to show our best side to the world and to celebrate diversity with the great and good. Politically, it is very useful to be able to offer a low-effort way for Jewish leaders and the wider great and good to make nice. Let's face it, very few of those who grace public candle-lightings with their august presence are aware of the ironies of using a deeply particularist festival for faux-universalist ends. I'm not sure many would even care if they did know. Chanukah is just too useful for all concerned.

Then there's Christmas. Chanukah allows Jews to join the party, at least to an extent. The Christmasification of Chanukah stems partially from the irresistible desire of many Jews in the postwar capitalist world to take part in the consumerist revels. There is, in fact, an older tradition of giving presents of money (specifically coins, for their light-reflecting qualities), so it's not much of a stretch to join in with the gift-giving. Chanukah Christmasified goes at least some way to assuage the temptations of joining in with the nominally Christian materialist fun. For non-Jews, Chanukah is easily assimilated into the festive calendar – we do Christmas, they do Chanukah, Hindus do Diwali and so on. Public Jews rarely rush to disabuse non-Jews of the conflation of these rituals with very different roots and meanings. After all, on paper there should be an impossible gap between a festival celebrating the birth of the saviour of humanity and one celebrating a bunch of awkward Jews preserving their right to be Jews. Even in secular terms, the orgiastic celebration of Christmas hardly compares with the doughnut-based celebration of Chanukah.

In private, there is scope for reflecting on these ironies. When Jews light the menorah in the same room as the Christmas tree, it's not as though the Jewish celebrants don't notice the juxtaposition. Such acts can feel ridiculous, slyly subversive, sacrilegious, hypocritical and tremendous fun at the same time. 'Chrismakah' is most definitely a thing. The problem, though, is when Jews are ignorant of – or simply choose not to reflect on – the depth of the irony. When Jews don't know or don't want to know how profoundly different Chanukah and Christmas are, any subversive potential is lost. The same is true when public Jews don't acknowledge that public celebrations of Chanukah in non-Jewish spaces involve a certain amount of pretence. Too often it is the Jews who end up fooling themselves, rather than the Jews manipulating the non-Jews.

Who is in charge of the process of making Chanukah a public festival? I fear we might have lost control of it. Frankly, there was something quite sad about the quote with which I started this chapter. That two rabbis 'were at different Chanukah events every night of the festival' made me wonder when they actually got to celebrate the festival. There is a very thin line between using Chanukah to demonstrate that public Jews have a seat at the top table, and public Jews being wheeled out at event after event to enable public bodies to show how inclusive they are.

In these kinds of events, Chanukah can't even just be fun, there has to be some kind of bigger purpose. In 2021, the newly formed Jewish Supporters Group for the football team I support – Watford FC – held a Chanukah party. The press release from the club gave a flavour of the revels:

> The guests heard speeches from Lord Mann of Holbeck Moor, the Government's Independent Adviser on Anti-Semitism, Edleen John, Director for International Relations, Corporate Affairs, and Equality, Diversity and Inclusion at the FA [Football Association], and Tony Burnett, Chief Executive of Kick it Out [a charity that combats racism in football].[5]

The contribution that Lord Mann (who isn't a Watford supporter, or Jewish) made to the event is described as follows:

> Lord Mann was first to speak and gave a glowing tribute to the group, saying: 'This evening is a chance for the Watford fans to congratulate and celebrate not only their club, but also the Jewish Hornets supporters' group on the important work that they are doing to combat anti-semitism and

to highlight the club's adoption of the IHRA definition of anti-semitism.'

True, there was also candle lighting, singing and messages from players. But the prominent speechifying against antisemitism gave the event a serious purpose that it didn't need to have. Why not just celebrate? Why couldn't an event held by a group of supporters of a fairly mediocre club be as insular and partisan as football fandom itself?

In recent years, a horrible thought has started to dawn on me: What if the Jewish organisers of public Chanukah celebrations really believe that these events are genuinely opportunities to celebrate multicultural harmony? What if the public Jews who flit between public Chanukah celebrations are *not* being cynical? What if the beaming smiles of the Jewish great and good in the press releases are genuine smiles?

It seems unthinkable – or at least it does to me – but Jewish public politics has, in recent decades, been transformed in ways that our ancestors could barely have imagined.

Things have gotten a bit weird

Adam Sandler's 'Chanukah song', quoted in Chapter Three, is framed as offering comfort to 'the only kid in town' who doesn't celebrate Christmas, by offering a list of fellow Jews. So it is that Christmas embodies our anxiety about our small numbers and minority presence. Sandler is not the only one to engage in such light-hearted responses to Jewish exclusion from Christmas – think, for example, of Kyle Broflowski's song 'A Lonely Jew at Christmas' in *South Park* – but there is something very strange about how Sandler offers comfort. While the song does mention celebrities who are not widely known as Jewish and have partial Jewish ancestry (such as Harrison Ford), the bulk of the lyrics appear to 'out' Jews who are widely known to be Jewish. The song demonstrates to the hypothetically lonely Jew at Christmas that we are much more numerous than we might seem, yet the ease with which he finds examples of openly Jewish celebrities undermines the entire premise of the song.

'Chanukah Song' offers a strange kind of Jewification: While 'classic' Jewification desperately draws on the most tenuous examples of Jewishness in order to make the world seem filled with it, Adam Sandler seeks to offer consolation to the anxiety of Jewish absence by pointing to some of the best-known Jews in the world. For Sandler, Chanukah's high public profile – so high that he first performed it on *Saturday Night Live,* a show with a very prominent Jewish history – is not *enough.* Or maybe he is pretending it isn't enough or parodying that desire for more; either way, the song's popularity with American Jews suggests that it resonates.

We seem to want contradictory things: Ubiquitous presence and ineffable marginality, total assimilation and complete otherness, proud publicity and private obscurity. In the US, the UK and other Diaspora communities, Chanukah embodies this confused Jewish yearning. This might seem like a harmless enough phenomenon, but it is connected to a kind of Jewish politics that has serious consequences.

In the US, UK and many other (but not all) countries, something extraordinary happened in the post-war period. In the decades after the Second World War it became possible for Jews to live lives in which antisemitism was not a serious threat. True, there were many caveats: this process happened unevenly and at different rates depending on what sort of Jew you were and where you lived; in some countries, such as the Soviet Union and its satellites plus most Islamic countries, it didn't happen at all; the vulnerability of the state of Israel did cause anxiety in the Diaspora too. Still, by the 1990s, it had become possible for many Diaspora Jews to expect to never be the object of overt discrimination or the worst kinds of abuse.

The 1990s was also a time when the state of Israel had developed to the point when it seemed less vulnerable. This might seem an odd point to make in a decade that saw Saddam Hussein lobbing missiles at the country in 1991, the assassination of Yitzhak Rabin in 1995 and sporadic Palestinian suicide bombings. Yet that decade also saw the country become a much more convivial place for Diaspora Jews to visit or to engage with from afar. The liberalisation of the Israeli economy and the integration of Israel into the post-1989 world of triumphant capitalism meant the country lost its rough-and-ready, work-in-progress feel. The Oslo accords and the famous handshake between Rabin and Arafat on the White House lawn in 1993 – benevolently supervised by Bill Clinton – meant that liberal Jews abroad could justifiably hope for an Israel that would lose its nerve-racking edginess.

In the 1990s it was possible for the mass of liberally minded Jews in the US, UK and some other Diaspora countries to feel that Jewish history was turning in their favour. That's one of the reasons why in the US and the UK, much effort was spent on professionalising, renewing and innovating within Jewish organisations; with antisemitism and threats to Israel receding, there was the space to look inward. At the same time, in an apparent paradox, greater comfort and security allowed Jews to speak of insecurity, of pain and trauma. The 1990s saw a flourishing of Holocaust memorialisation and remembrance. The post-communist states of Eastern Europe and the Former Soviet Union became more open to the building of memorials and educational tours. In the US, the Holocaust Museum in Washington, DC finally opened after years of planning;

museums and memorials mushroomed across the world, including in post-wall Berlin. By the 2000s, Holocaust memorial days had been instituted in many European countries. Jews were able to push for such public recognition with confidence and without shame.

What is extraordinary is how quickly Jews got used to this highly atypical set of historical circumstances. We can see how accustomed we became to a benign Jewish existence in some of the reactions to war in Israel and antisemitism in the Diaspora post-7 October 2023. For example, in London, where I live, it has been striking to observe how some Jewish organisations and public figures have reacted to the regular pro-Palestinian marches held in the centre of the city. It is not surprising that many Jews have found these marches intimidating, particularly since they often contain a contingent of militants that tacitly or openly support Hamas. What is more surprising is the incredulity that such protests should be happening at all. The *Jewish Chronicle* and other publications published article after article expressing outrage at pro-Palestinian demonstrations, such as this one by Stephen Pollard from February 2024:

> Every week, for example, mobs of hundreds of thousands take to our streets with genocidal screams of 'From the river to the sea', chanting support of the Houthis, parading posters that could have come straight from Nazi Germany, and demanding jihad and global intifada.
>
> And what do the authorities do? They stand and watch as these hate marches take over London – and other cities – and turn them into no-go areas for Jews. The marches – despite their repeated, clear and proud intent – are given the go-ahead by a police force which has lost the will and the ability to keep the streets free from hate.[6]

While there have certainly been hateful contingents at pro-Palestinian demonstrations, articles such as Pollard's homogenise the protestors, ruling out *a priori* that any one of them could be motivated by simple concern for lives lost in Gaza. More importantly, they demonstrate totally unrealistic expectations. Frankly, it would have been astonishing if a significant chunk of public opinion didn't see the terrible suffering in Gaza as, at the very least, a more pressing priority than those in Israel who suffered on 7 October and its aftermath. It would be even more bizarre if Israel, militarily far and away the strongest party, attracted the kind of sympathy that an 'underdog' usually attracts. I am not making an argument here on the justice or otherwise of Israel's cause; only pointing out the inevitability that opposition to Israel will be a popular cause in these circumstances and that those who embrace that cause are not all motivated by antisemitism.

There was a time when Jews might have been more phlegmatic. The state of Israel was founded and spent its first few decades in the teeth of global suspicion and hostility. Even those states who supported Israel's recognition and supplied arms to it were not necessarily motivated by love of the new state. There were good geopolitical reasons for Western countries to ally with Israel, but the Jewish state never got a blank cheque. As late as 1992, President George H.W. Bush withheld loan guarantees until he received assurances that the money would not go to settlements, unimaginable for any Republican president today. When Diaspora Jews set out to defend Israel and make its case, it was without any automatic assumption of success.

The same was true for antisemitism. These days, many Jewish organisations call for a 'zero tolerance' approach to antisemitism. It's a worthy goal and a totally impractical one. It leads us to conflate incidents that earlier generations of Jews would barely have noticed with incidents that any Jew in any generation would be traumatised by. How quickly we got used to not being hated!

Jews have millennia of experience of surviving, and often thriving, in a world in which we are only a tiny fragment. That includes the vital skill of ensuring that we can carry on existing amid the constantly changing morass of power politics. When a ruler looked upon us kindly, we always knew that we would have to hedge our bets against the day when a new regime took hold. After all, in verse 1:8 of the book of Exodus, we are told that 'there arose a new king over Egypt who did not know Joseph'. Moses, like countless Jewish leaders after him, had to finesse the survival of the people of Israel in inclement circumstances, ensuring by the narrowest of margins that we could escape.

Moses was one guy, and in some Jewish communities survival also depended on single individuals, representatives whose job it was to cajole and charm the ruler. In the modern world, though, Jewish political clout was boosted when Jews became citizens and a whole variety of leaders, movements and parties emerged, espousing a wide range of political ideologies. Socialists, communists, Zionists and liberal assimilationists may not have liked each other very much, but this Jewish plurality did allow for a kind of hedging of political bets; if one party didn't appeal to the ruling government, another one might. And while in catastrophic circumstances like the Holocaust it was all for naught, the plurality of the modern Jewish political imagination did engender an awareness that Jews could be political.

The post-war period saw the erosion of this plurality as liberal forms of Zionism became normative in most Diaspora communities, albeit with vociferous minorities on the far left and far right. One of the effects of this wide but not total consensus was, as I have argued elsewhere, a 'forgetting of the Jewish political tradition'.[7] It wasn't just that anti-Zionists were frequently turned into pariahs; Jewish leaders and organisations became unwilling and unable to argue for Zionism as one political ideology competing among other political ideologies.

By the 1990s a dangerous assumption had begun to spread – that Jewish survival depended on friendship, likeability and even love. The grinning faces of Jews and non-Jews at public Chanukah candle-lightings are just one example of this emphasis on building convivial relationships. This is not a phenomenon confined to one part of the political spectrum. Jewish anti-Zionists get it on with pro-Palestinian campaigners at protest marches just as Jewish far-right activists cuddle up with Islamophobic campaigners. In the UK, one of the most striking aspects of the controversy over antisemitism in the Labour Party under the leadership of Jeremy Corbyn (2015–20) was the mobilisation of opposing Jewish factions to accuse or defend the leader and his party. These Jewish factions drew on longstanding friendships with non-Jewish allies and replayed longstanding, equally personal enmities with opponents. Jeremy Corbyn was supported by Jews he had been friends with for decades; the same was true for the embattled right of the party, which deepened equally longstanding relationships with Jewish Labour activists.

This isn't politics. This is a love-in. If the fate of the Jews depends on people loving us, then we really are screwed.

We are loved, in part, because we are important. Outside of old-style neo-Nazis and militant Islamists, Jews have become more than Jews. On the pro-Palestinian left we are loved for our radical tradition and hated when Zionist Jews appear to traduce that tradition. On the Islamophobic right we are loved for holding the frontline against the Islamic hordes. In the liberal centre – the space that still attracts most Jews in the US, UK and many other Diaspora countries – we must be cherished because antisemitism is a threat to democracy itself. As Jonathan Sacks, the late Chief Rabbi of the UK, argued in a speech to the European Parliament in 2016:

> The hate that begins with Jews never ends with Jews. We make a great mistake if we think antisemitism is a threat only to Jews. It is a threat, first and foremost, to Europe and to the freedoms it took centuries to achieve.

It is easy to see how such arguments might resonate in Europe, particularly in countries where the Holocaust was carried out. The European Union's 'Strategy on Combating Antisemitism and Fostering Jewish Life (2021–2030)' begins with Sacks's quote and goes on to state unequivocally:

> Antisemitism is incompatible with Europe's core values. It represents a threat not only to Jewish communities and to Jewish life, but to an open and diverse society, to democracy and the European way of life. The European Union is determined to put an end to it.[8]

Such aspirations are laudable. Societies where antisemitism is tolerated tend to be societies where many other freedoms are threatened. The primacy that Sacks accords to antisemitism is empirically dubious, though; the world abounds with many kinds of hate, as it has always done, and to give one hate a greater causal power than another is unsustainable from a historical or sociological point of view. Moreover, when the condition of the Jewish people becomes a major – or *the* major – yardstick to measure the wider condition of societies, we risk becoming

symbols for something other than ourselves; we become freedom and democracy itself. Love freedom? Love the Jews.

Let's get cynical, cynical, I want to get cynical

If the struggle against antisemitism is also a struggle for something much larger, then it risks neglecting an important set of
tools that can help grease the anti-racist wheel: Political tools,
wielded cynically. A 'full-spectrum' fight against a complex phenomenon like antisemitism requires more than guiding values;
it also requires calculation and making antisemites an offer they
can't refuse. Not all antisemites are persuadable and some anti-
semitisms go too deep to be shifted, but we shouldn't neglect
the possibility that antisemitism can be fought through appeals
to self-interest. What offer could we make that might be better
than antisemitism? How could we make a persuasive case that
one could forgo antisemitism without having to sign up to a
wearisome set of values?

Well, actually, some non-Jews are acting as if that offer has
already been made. There is an ever-growing vein of self-interested anti-antisemitism, embraced for a variety of reasons. The
problem is that Jews' ability to spot this kind of opposition to
antisemitism is variable. Increasingly we seem to have drunk
our own Kool-Aid. Far too often, when we see opposition to
antisemitism, we seem to act as though it is a moving gesture of
support by people who care for us. We shower our 'allies' with
awards and invite them to our Chanukah parties. We smile and
return the love.

Sometimes we are right to see our defenders this way. There
are good people in the world, after all, and some of them take
fighting antisemitism as their mission. The problem is that we
don't actually know who they are. There is a Hasidic concept
of the *Tzadikim Nistarim*, the 'hidden righteous'; there are 36

and the fate of the world depends on them. We cannot know them because we humans cannot scan the contents of people's hearts. While that means we shouldn't automatically suspect the motivations of our friends, we should also not take them at face value, either. Jews need to hold something of ourselves back. Right now we are at risk of going all in.

One example of how acute this risk can be is the struggle over the IHRA (International Holocaust Remembrance Alliance) definition of antisemitism. Most 'mainstream' Jewish representative bodies across the world advocate its adoption by public bodies. It has been fiercely criticised by pro-Palestinian activists and by many Jewish intellectuals (not just anti-Zionist ones) on a number of grounds, most importantly that it delegitimises criticism of Israel to such an extent that it risks eroding freedom of speech and pro-Palestinian advocacy. Its strongest advocates and strongest critics often share an assumption that when an institution decides to adopt or not adopt IHRA, that's the end of the story; either that institution is now 'safe' for Jews or it is 'hostile' to Palestinians and other critics of Israel. As I have argued elsewhere, adopting IHRA doesn't actually mean very much in terms of how it will be applied in practice (for example, in disciplinary procedures within a particular institution).[9] We know almost nothing beyond anecdote about how IHRA is actually being used 'in the field', nor does there seem much appetite to conduct systematic research on this issue. It is entirely possible – even likely – that many institutions who have made decisions to adopt or not adopt IHRA have done it for self-interested reasons. Depending on the institution, it can be a no-brainer to throw a bone to the Jews, or, conversely, to Palestinians and their advocates, by jumping on or off the IHRA bandwagon. At any rate, those who support that decision are unlikely to ask any awkward questions about what adoptees will actually do with the definition.

The Watford FC Chanukah party shows the benefits of adopting IHRA. Adopt it and you get a member of the House of Lords bigging you up and lots of happy Jews. What's not to like? The Jews and government envoys seem to believe that adoption of IHRA is an idealistic and sympathetic gesture by non-Jews who care for us. Why disabuse them? In fact, it might even be the true motivation. The problem is, we will never know.

Sometimes it's fine to use people and to be used in return. Cynicism can be a way of achieving idealistic goals. But you have to know that that is what you are doing. If you 'forget' that you are acting instrumentally, cynicism becomes one-way; Jews get used and that can lead to abuse.

In my 2019 book *Strange Hate*, I drew attention to a phenomenon I called 'selective' antisemitism. Selective antisemitism combines love for one kind of Jew with hate (or, at least, dislike) for another kind of Jew. Such selectivity is particularly prevalent on the far left and far right. IHRA can play a part here too. Notably, while Viktor Orbán's Hungary has often used antisemitic discourse against George Soros and other such 'globalist' Jews, many of its public bodies have also adopted IHRA. An apparent gesture of 'love' towards Jews is adopted as indemnification against criticism from a certain kind of Jew. There are also many equivalents of this selectivity on the left. The care with which some pro-Palestinian activists distinguish Jews and Zionists is, in fact, a selective gesture that excludes Jews who have the wrong politics from protection unless they are attacked by full-blown Nazis (and sometimes not even then). Given our diversity, it is pretty easy to find Jews to defend you and those Jews will be happy to be wielded as a weapon against the bad Jews.

Such instrumentalising of Jews extends beyond self-defence against accusations of antisemitism. In his 2018 polemic *De-Integrate!* the German-Jewish writer Max Czollek castigated the use that some Germans make of Jews.[10] As he argued, 'the public role of Jews has existed to affirm the German Redemption Story in the German "Theatre of Memory"'. Within this performative space – in books, speeches, museums and memorials – 'The Good German needs the Good Jew as counterpart – a figure so saccharine sweet that one could never imagine them containing even a single drop of unforgiveness in their veins.' The presence of Jews in Germany becomes a kind of legitimation for the claim that the Germany of today is not the 'other' Germany of the past.

Czollek's polemic is harsh and sometimes unfair. There are many Germans for whom redemption is a hard path and restitution more than a matter of exculpatory memorials. Nevertheless, Czollek highlights just how easily apparently philosemitic gestures can become self-serving and can end up having nothing much to do with real living Jews. A few years after his book was published, a major controversy broke in Germany regarding Rabbi Walter Homolka, founder and at the time rector of Abraham Geiger College in Potsdam.[11] The College was founded in 1999 to train progressive rabbis and had received very significant public funds over the years, raised almost entirely by Homolka. The controversy began in 2022 when allegations were made that he had tolerated his husband's alleged sexual harassment of students. It quickly grew into a much wider debate about Homolka's alleged abuses of power. This included the astonishing fact that he owned the College legally, accusations that he had bullied and abused students, that he exercised effective control over German progressive Jewry, that his rabbinic ordination was questionable, and that he might have engaged in academic malpractice.[12] Homolka's success depended to a great extent on his formidable ability to make connections and extract money from the German establishment, together with the relatively weak state of German Jewish institutions that might have resisted him. A 2023 article on the scandal by the American author Laura Moser included the following cutting quotes:[13]

> 'Homolka's pitch was "I can give you this new Jew, who is liberal and not too different, who unlike all these Ludmillas and Tatianas and Mikhaels speaks great German,"' says a rabbinic student who eventually left Abraham Geiger College after being harassed by Homolka's partner for several years. 'He also doesn't come with the trauma or any sense of danger about Germany, or any of the reservations that the Jews who lived in Germany before 1990 had.'
>
> 'His was a Judaism that didn't hurt the German Protestant prejudices,' says Christoph Schulte of the University of Potsdam's Jewish Studies Department, who has written pieces critical of Homolka. 'He was, in rabbinical costume, the non-Jew's convenient projection of those assimilated, bourgeois liberal German Jews we lost in the Shoah. A Biergarten Jew.'

The Homolka scandal (which, at the time of writing, is only partially resolved) is an example of how, when it comes to Jews, cynicism and idealism can become entangled. The Germans whom he charmed were at once paying for redemption at a very competitive price and also working to support Jewish life in Germany, thereby redeeming a country with a dark past. The Jews who supported Homolka were hitching their wagon to a man who could raise vast sums of cash and who offered a tempting vision of a reborn Jewish community.

The Homolka scandal, as well as the wider issues with German Jewry raised by Max Czollek, are further signs that the Jewish capacity for cynicism has eroded in the last few decades. Too often, what at first sight may appear to be demonstrations of Jewish political skill end up as demonstrations of how cheaply we can be bought. The title of this chapter is ironic; even though we mislead non-Jews every Chanukah, we are in many ways the swindled rather than the swindler. In the guise of being proud public Jews who fight our corner, too often we are simply moulding ourselves for public approval.

As I suggested in the previous chapters, our capacity for mediocrity means that we are usually not very good at being secret manipulators. We attempt to manipulate openly and thereby have become a prime target to be manipulated. Contrary to Ilhan Omar's tweet from 2019, the apparent Jewish success in securing US support for Israel was never 'all about the Benjamins', at least not entirely. In Jewish politics, what appears like 'buying' support may have more to do with politicians and public bodies barely believing their good fortune in being able to get the Jews off their back with hardly any effort, often doing what they would be doing anyway.

In any case, our lack of cynicism can be politically self-defeating. I wrote this chapter in the summer of 2024 while following the turmoil in Columbia University and other US universities caused by pro-Palestinian demonstrations. Much of the Jewish world was reacting with horror, with a significant minority in the reverse. When observers point out that there are, in fact, multiple factions among the protestors, Jewish opponents barely reacted and Jewish supporters conversely ignored the more problematic elements. As far as I can see, no one in mainstream Jewish communal organisations seemed to be doing the obvious and cynical thing: Surreptitiously manipulating latent tensions among the protestors, dividing and ruling, paying off the payoffable. That refusal led to a zero-sum politics that can only be successful if all pro-Palestinian protest everywhere at anytime is suppressed, violently if necessary. Some may want that, but it isn't going to happen; there will always be a campus somewhere in America where protest would continue to flourish.

To be clear, I do not wish to see such suppression; I don't wish to see Jewish organisations adopting the cynical policy I suggest. What I do want to see is Diaspora Jewish populations recognising that cynicism and politics exist in the world and that there is no shame in acknowledging it. Actually, we should hope that those we deal with are cynical too; that way we can speak a language of mutual self-interest. Maybe then we might be able to get things done.

Chapter Nine
The Israel chapter

Opinions

It's really pretty irrelevant what I think of Israel.

There is no shortage of people, Jewish and non-Jewish, who have Opinions on the subject. Whatever you might think about Israel or Palestine, there will be a bloc of people, led by people with Opinions, who think the same. Some of them might even be Israeli or Palestinian.

One result of events since 7 October 2023 has been a kind of irrevocable decision-making across the board. While Israel–Palestine has been one of the most contested issues in the world for many years now, the sheer extremity of both Hamas' assault and the Israeli response has eaten into the ranks of the undecided. One way or another, it's become much harder not to have Opinions, to decide what you actually think, to choose enemies and heroes.

That decision-making has been particularly profound on the left. However entangled the relationship between Jews and left politics might have been since the nineteenth century, we seem to have reached a point of no return when it comes to tolerance for Israel. The Gaza war, and what many leftists see as a genocide, will not be forgiven or forgotten. A significant chunk of the world will never reconcile themselves to Israel in any form. The huge protests, sit-ins and acts of civil disobedience are likely to constitute defining events in the lives of those who took part in them.

For Jews who participate in the Jewish blocs in the protests, this will also be a defining moment. After decades of marginalisation, there is no longer any hiding the fact that not all Jews support Israel and Zionism. In contrast, for those Jews in the Diaspora who support the existence of Israel, this period will be remembered as a nightmare. The demonstrations will be remembered as intimidating expressions of hate and antisemitism, the Jewish presence on them a kick in the teeth from the young and easily exploited. Israel will never have seemed more vulnerable, more hated, yet also more needed as a refuge.

Of course, the decided co-exist with the conflicted: Zionists who cannot support military actions that lead to so many civilian deaths do exist, as do Palestinians who condemn Hamas for unleashing hell on 7 October 2023, as do protestors with no previous connection to Israel or Palestine who took to the streets out of simple empathy with the Gazan dead. But right now, and for the foreseeable future, it is the decided who are making the running and making history. Indeed, a major theme in the discourse is to 'pick a side' since 'silence is complicity'.

One of the ironies of this endemic decision-making is that the situation on the ground is so fluid, so unpredictable, that it is a terrible place to ground oneself in certainty. That goes for writers of non-fiction books too. Throughout the writing and editing of this book, I tore my hair out wondering how I could 'future proof' this text so that my arguments could remain relevant for at least a few years. I am painfully aware that, while this book was conceived and written against the backdrop of 7 October 2023 and the war in Gaza, I couldn't rule out a near future in which this disaster might be relegated to a mild curtain raiser for an even greater disaster.

Against this backdrop, is there even any point in me talking about Israel? Actually, never mind me, is there a point to anyone talking about Israel?

I think there is, but it needs to be a different kind of conversation. Regardless of what Israel–Palestine looks like when this book is published, what is unlikely to change for many years is the constant projection onto Israelis and Palestinians of any and every agenda. If we can find a way to unpick the endless entanglement of Israel in fantasies, dreams, nightmares and hope, we might be able to find not the 'real' Israel, but an Israel that might be more resistant to such projections.

Naturally, the place to start is with the queen of Israeli television advertising.

My recommendation

In the late 1990s and early 2000s, I kept seeing something odd on Israeli TV. During those years I spent extended periods in the country, not as an immigrant, but to undertake research for my PhD and then to participate in a fellowship programme. Israeli TV fascinated me, although my Hebrew is of variable quality and I didn't always understand what I was seeing. But it wasn't the language issues that were baffling me. Rather, it was that the *same woman* seemed to be advertising many different products in the same way over many different adverts, even using the same music. She sung the praises of breakfast cereal, processed meat, mortgage providers, washing powder – pretty much anything you can think of.

One example saw the woman – who appeared to be in late middle-age – standing in the kitchen, holding up a packet and beaming over a boy and a girl (perhaps supposed to be her grandchildren?) devouring chocolate cake. In an insistent and commanding voice, she declaimed to camera:

Kids love chocolate cake but they go crazy over *chocolaty* chocolate cake!

New! Self-raising flour by Osem especially made for chocolate cake. More chocolaty and much more tasty. Keep the recipe you love and switch the flour to chocolate-flavoured self-raising flour and taste chocolate cake with the real taste of chocolate.

My recommendation: Osem self-raising flour with chocolate flavouring for rich and chocolaty cake.

She finished by reciting Osem's dull-as-dishwater slogan:

It's good, it's Osem![1]

Most of her ads were like this: The suggestion of domestic-goddesshood, obsessive repetition of adjectives (chocolaty chocolate!) and the climactic 'my recommendation'. The style is no-nonsense; there is a brutal shamelessness in her insistence that we buy that product.

Who was she? Israeli friends all knew her and told me her story, sometimes rolling their eyes, sometimes laughing affectionately. She is known as G Yafit (or just 'Gimmel', the name of the letter 'g' in Hebrew), although her full name is Yafit Greenberg. She was born in 1951 into a Libyan-Jewish family, one of those who were expelled or fled following Israeli independence in 1948. She spent most of her career in advertising and marketing before her death from cancer in 2021. A formidable woman, Gimmel owned her own advertising agency and, a few years before her death, she was wealthy enough to buy the Israeli bookstore chain Steimatsky. She started off in newspaper advertising, and when commercial TV began in Israel in the early 1990s she spotted an opportunity; by making and fronting TV adverts herself, she could offer a competitive price to manufacturers of any and every product.

When Israel's defenders talk of explaining the 'real Israel', it's not Gimmel that they are thinking of. When Diaspora Jewish youngsters are taught about Israel, Gimmel is not part of the standard curriculum. When pro-Palestinian activists point to the disgrace that is Israel, it's not Gimmel's clunky ads that they are thinking of. She exists in a mutual blind spot, well-known in Israel and beloved in a so-bad-it's-good kind of way, but completely outside the narratives and fantasies in which Israel is enmeshed.

While Gimmel's oeuvre is one of unrelenting mediocrity, she herself was an extraordinary woman. The question is whether her extraordinariness was related to her Jewish Israeliness.

In some respects she was an 'only in Israel' figure, an example of how Jews from Arab lands overcame discrimination and destitution after immigrating to or being expelled to Israel in the 1950s. In other respects, she could be from anywhere. Someone somewhere was always likely to have the brainwave of offering near-identical adverts presented by the same perma-grinning shill to anyone that will pay. It just happened that it was an Israeli woman who had the brainwave. In fact, not having an encyclopaedic knowledge of TV advertising around the world, I can't rule out the possibility that maybe there is a Gimmel Yafit elsewhere, or maybe loads of them.

It's the Gimmels who make a nation. They are the ones who struggle, in extraordinary ways, to create the conditions in which mediocre everydayness can flourish. The extraordinary Jewish state has enabled an unprecedented extension of Jewish mundanity. Whereas in the Diaspora, today or in the past, Jewish life required that Jews engage with a wider field of everyday mediocrity, Jews didn't run the sewage system or make many of the products for sale in shops and markets. A Jewish state enables a 'full spectrum' mediocrity in which life can be lived within a cocoon of Jewish not-particularly goodness.

Much of this mediocrity is viewed affectionately in Israel while baffling outsiders. One example is Bamba, the wildly popular peanut-butter-flavoured puffed-maize snack that forms an integral part of any Israeli childhood. That includes children with peanut allergies, as other flavours do exist, including strawberry, unforgivably. Many countries have snacks of this kind – in the UK, Wotsits are its closest equivalent – but the peanut-butter flavouring seems more unique. It's an acquired taste that I personally haven't acquired. To us Bamba refuseniks, the peanut-butter flavouring lends the puffed maize a disconcerting dryness; the mouth yearns for lubrication. Bamba is exported to the Diaspora and you often find it, for example, at independence day celebrations. Yet tastebuds may overwhelm Zionist feeling. At my son's Jewish school there was a running battle between UK-born kids like him and Israel-born pupils over whether Bamba is horrible or not. To fail to appreciate Bamba seems an insult. Indeed, so taken-for-granted is the assumption that Bamba is a delight, Palestinians have been punished with the withholding of it: In 2009, while the Israeli soldier Gilad Shalit was being held hostage in Gaza, an Israeli army official responsible for vetting what food could be brought into Gaza explained, 'We don't want Gilad Shalit's captors to be munching Bamba right over his head.'[2]

. When Israel's defenders defend the Jewish state online, on TV, in print and at public debates, they do not mention Bamba or Gimmel Yafit as justifications for Israel's existence. The 'case for Israel' can be made in various ways according to the audience – historical justice, fighting the Muslim hordes, the only democracy in the region, Tel Aviv as a gay-friendly city, shows on Netflix, Nobel Prize winners, the 'start-up nation', cute female soldiers with machine guns, etc., etc. Everyday mediocrity is not a weapon in this arsenal. This front is unguarded. Pro-Palestinian activists (and Palestinians themselves) are not going to see peanut-butter-flavoured maize puffs as justification for everything else.

The sociologist Michael Billig has called the everyday ways in which a sense of shared nationhood is built 'banal nationalism'.[3] The nation is built and its identity reinforced through a myriad of small, seemingly inconsequential details – and that includes snack products and celebrities. At the same time, this banality is only used sparingly and inconsistently as an argument for the existence of a particular nation. Somehow the banal is not 'enough'; it is treated as at best a by-product of the 'soul' of the nation, not its creator. Gimmel and those extraordinary immigrants like her are sometimes treated as part of that soul. The crap she flogged is ignored. That's as true in Israel as it is in many other countries, but the banality that sustains Israel also raises uncomfortable questions which the Zionist project has long wrestled with but never resolved.

Are we normal yet?

Yehuda Amichai's well-known 1971 poem 'Tourists' bemoans the disconnection between visitors to his country from everyday Israeli life and everyday Israelis.[4] It ends by recalling an occasion where he sat next to David's Tower in Jerusalem with two heavy shopping bags. A tour guide uses him as a 'target marker', pointing out to his group that, to the right of the man with the baskets, there's an arch from the Roman period. Amichai reflects that 'redemption' will come when a tour guide points out that, to the left of a Roman arch, there's a man who has bought fruit and vegetables for his family.

The poem speaks of a yearning for an Israel that is just a place where people live, not one that bears the burden of history; a 'normal' place, in other words. At the same time, the desire expressed in the poem is for everyday, regular Israels – like Amichai himself – to be recognised as worthy of note. That suggests a surreptitious ambivalence. If Amichai had wanted normality so badly, then his career was a complete failure. A pioneering figure in the development of modern Hebrew literature, winner of multiple prizes in Israel and around the world, the holder of fistfuls of honorary doctorates, he is one example of the extraordinary achievement of the Zionist movement to build not just a state, but also a culture of global significance.

One of the most famous quotes in Zionist history is by David Ben-Gurion, the first prime minister of the country: 'When Israel has prostitutes and thieves, we'll be a state just like any other.' As in Amichai's poem, there is a hidden self-subversion here; Ben-Gurion defines normality through the existence of vice and crime, not through the dull routines of everyday existence. In any case, Ben-Gurion himself wasn't very good at being mundane. His house in Tel Aviv, now preserved as a museum, is festooned with books in multiple languages and displays part of his voluminous correspondence. Like many other early Zionists, he was a thinker as well as a doer, obsessed with trying to define what this new nation should be and what kind of solidarity would hold it together.

Another renowned Israeli intellectual, A.B. Yehoshua, extolled 'normality' as the goal of the state of Israel and the Zionist movement. In the Diaspora, Jews cannot live a normal life as Jews, even with no antisemitism; the condition of Diaspora compromises the possibility of a 'total' Jewish existence.[5] Yet how normal can existence – Jewish or otherwise – be if it is only possible on one particular patch of land? If a Jewish state of Israel holds the only possibility of normalising the Jewish condition, then it makes Jews abnormal among the nations of the world, where Diasporas are commonplace. Would anyone argue that one can only be a normal Chinese person in China?

The prospect that Israel will be treated as a normal state is fiercely resisted in the pro-Palestinian movement worldwide. To normalise Israel would be to normalise the *naqba* and the ongoing oppression of the Palestinians. Attempts to institute Boycotts, Divestment and Sanctions (BDS) against Israeli goods, society and culture are attempts to insist on the impossibility of treating even the most mundane aspects of Israel as unconnected to its crimes. Everything connected to Israel is irredeemably extraordinary. What such practices don't acknowledge is that Israel might not want normalisation either.

The ambivalence of Israeli intellectuals towards normalisation reflects something important about the nation-building process that is very hard to accept: It's actually quite easy and it's usually disappointing.

Disappointing normality

Israel was born out of intellectual ferment. The pre-state Zionist movement constituted itself through journals, books and intense arguments. Those who settled the country built opera houses, universities, publishers, newspapers and art galleries. Some of the greatest minds in Jewish history participated in this extraordinary process, from Gershom Scholem to Martin Buber. The implication of all of this was that a Jewish nation state could not simply be brought into being by Jewish immigration, kibbutzes, military insurgency and diplomatic efforts; Israel had to be *thought* into being too.

This intellectual effort was necessary to make a modern Jewish nation state a 'thinkable' prospect. Yearning for Zion has been a part of Jewish life since the destruction of the second temple in 70 CE, and there was a near-continual Jewish presence in the land itself, sometimes augmented by modest numbers of immigrants. Recasting Zion as a modern nation state required confronting the huge gap between ancient Jewish models of sovereignty and models of the contemporary nation state. A major part of that work was the audacious transformation of Hebrew as a language of liturgy and literature, into an everyday tongue that Jews from every part of the world could learn. That work didn't just require the 'creation' of modern Hebrew by intellectuals – most notably, Eliezer Ben-Yehuda – it also required writers and speakers to experiment with the new tongue, its possibilities and limitations. Modern Hebrew poets like Bialik and Zelda were not just engaged in literature for its own sake, they were creating a nation through its language.

Even though the life of the mind was essential to making the Jewish state of Israel a viable proposition, its consolidation owed as much, if not more, to more mundane activities. The Zionist movement in pre-state Palestine didn't just produce learned journals; it created the infrastructure of a modern state in parallel to and often in conflict with the British mandate powers. That meant trade unions, welfare organisations, city authorities, domestic utility companies and the like, all bound together with complex bureaucracies. Although the dominant current within Zionism both before and after independence was Labour Zionism, with its statist orientation, the private sector also provided some of the building blocks of statehood. Osem, the company that makes Bamba, was founded in 1942 and focused on prosaic products like noodles, going on to produce Bamba in the 1960s. The company is now owned by Nestlé.

Such a conglomeration of mundane things cannot help but produce a nation. Just to live everyday life in Israel means shopping for Israeli products, paying taxes to the state, showering in water pumped by an Israeli utility company and trying to navigate the Israeli health system. Benedict Anderson, in his classic study *Imagined Communities*, showed how newly decolonised states such as Indonesia 'imagined' themselves into being in part through sharing a common bureaucracy.[6] Civil servants progressing up the hierarchy necessarily become conscious that there are others, sometimes competitors, who are doing the same. Through that sense that others in the same space as me are doing what I am doing, a self-conscious national community is built.

If all it takes to build a nation state is Bamba and bureaucracy, why are Israel and many other states so caught up in questions of what the nation should be? The problem is that while Bamba and bureaucracy may create a common sense of being part of a nation, that doesn't mean that everyone *wants* to be bound together in this way. Strictly orthodox Jews and Arab citizens of Israel have often had extremely tense relations with the Israeli state, even though they fill the coffers of Osem and pay their water bills. But even if you identify fervently with Israel, the mundane existence of Israel may simply not be 'enough'. Where's the drama? Where's the grand heroic narrative? Is the endpoint of the ancient Jewish struggle for survival the ability to buy unhealthy snackfood made by an Israeli subsidiary of a multinational corporation?

Of course, much of this dullness is counteracted by the dramatic and traumatic violent conflict in which Israel has always been embroiled. I am not arguing that Israel deliberately remains in a state of constant war as a way of staving off mundanity. In fact, there is a strong current within Israeli culture that responds to war with insouciance and just carries on. There can be a stark contrast between Israeli and Diaspora Jewish responses to Israel at war. On 13 April 2024, Iran launched volleys of missiles and drones towards Israel. During the hours between launch and arrival, my Jewish friends in the UK fretted and worried, drawing deeply on discourses of Israel as the embattled vanguard of the Jewish people. Many of my Israeli friends spent the time sharing and making humorous memes.[7] While humour is a common way for humans to deal with fear, it is striking how in this case it conflicted with the serious grand narratives that Israeli officials and the state's Diaspora defenders were weaving. Indeed, Israel's long tradition of political satire is often something that Israel's defenders ignore, as it doesn't really fit narratives of intense existential seriousness.

There is something about nationalism that resists the hopes placed in it, particularly when the creation and consolidation of the nation state demands so much blood. The heroic narratives that build the nation state risk bathos once the state is built. It isn't a surprise that, for many years now, one of the ascendant trends in Israeli politics has been religious Zionism. This has a long history, dating back to the pre-state era and the pioneering work of the Chief Rabbi Rav Kook to reconcile what was then an overwhelmingly secular movement with orthodox Judaism. In the wake of Israel's victory in the 1967 Six Day War, the project of settling the newly occupied territories became over time the most dynamic and vigorous movement within Zionism. The Israeli right, while not only religious, has had much less difficulty with disappointment than the liberal, left and secular parts of Israel. They offer a vision of a nation still being built, still expanding and still engaged in a redemptive process. While the rise of the Israel right isn't simply the result of the attractiveness of its vision (changing Israeli demographics are also part of the story), it does demonstrate that the vacuum that is left once nationalism succeeds can be filled by those who resist normality.

In any case, regardless of where Israelis and Diaspora Jewish Zionists might stand on the political spectrum, in PR terms it is hard to sell normality. Israel and its defenders emphasise the extraordinary aspects of the country and, in fairness, they have a lot of extraordinary stories to tell: Military and technological innovation, Nobel Prize winners, vibrant nightlife, robust civil society and much else. It is hard to square such stories with normality. Even when Israel does normal things they can be framed as extraordinary. For example, the 'Abraham Accords' process, which normalised relations with a number of Arab states from 2020 onwards, was driven to a large extent by a mutual desire to form a bloc against Iran and its proxies. It was often sold as a heartfelt process of reconciliation between the children of Abraham. For states to make alliances out of no other motive than reconciliation would be as ridiculous as it would be unlikely.

Not only is it difficult for Israelis and Diaspora Jews to accept the possibility of normality, however much they also yearn for it, the goalposts have shifted over time. There is no fixed standard of normality; it is subject to changing systems of values and politics. When Israel declared independence in 1948, it was one of many twentieth-century states who expelled potentially or actually 'hostile' populations outside their borders or refused to let wartime refugees return. Regardless of the morality, it was probably reasonable for Israel's leaders at the time to expect that the circumstances of Israel's foundation would be accepted and forgotten as were the expulsion of the Sudeten Germans from Czechoslovakia following the Second World War or the 'transfers' in Greece, Turkey and the Balkans following the First World War.

The reason why this normalisation never occurred is bitterly contested. Many Israelis and Diaspora Jews see this as a sign of antisemitic double standards. While one should want to see a world in which ethnic cleansing is condemned, it is also true that the everyday cynicism of most nation states often takes a holiday when it comes to Israel. One reason why the accusation of genocide made against Israel's actions in Gaza is so fiercely resisted is that, whether or not you agree with the charge, it will not be forgotten within a few years as many other genocides have been.

Perhaps Israelis are giving up on normality. That goes for the Israeli left too. Those Israelis who resist the occupation, who fight for a shared society, who opposed the destruction of Gaza, cannot rely on normal politics. When a right-wing government creates irrevocable facts on the ground – such as building a new settlement – biding one's time and hoping that the democratic pendulum will one day swing in your direction is a forlorn hope. That doesn't mean that the embattled Israeli left is giving up on democracy itself; it does mean they are making ever more extraordinary efforts to protest, to seek help abroad, to devote their lives to activism.

If normality isn't possible anymore, one can at least find a comfortable place amid its ruins in which to sit out the disaster. It's no coincidence that the extraordinary flowering of Israeli culture in recent years has taken place against the backdrop of despair. In the years following the outbreak of the second intifada in autumn 2000 and the death of the peace process, secular liberal Israelis began talking of *ha'bua,* the bubble. Within this bubble, young cosmopolitans in Tel Aviv frequented coffee shops, made out, sent texts, made art and enveloped themselves in a culture that 'caught up' with the world. While Israeli literature already had a high global profile, Israeli TV, film and music rarely left the country's borders. In fact, for all the dominance of Zionism in the Diaspora, young Israelis and young Diaspora Jews had limited common cultural reference points until relatively recently. Today, there are multiple Israeli dramas on Netflix, Spotify levels the playing field for Israeli rock, and films like *Waltz with Bashir* win prizes across the world.

Mediocrity lost

There was a time when Israel had mediocrity in spades. The first Israeli film I ever saw, *Lupo B'New York* ('Lupo Goes to New York'), was made in 1976 and tells the story of a loveable rag-and-bone man who misses his grandson when his family take a trip to New York. Lupo joins them in the Big Apple, leading to all sorts of 'hilarious' misunderstandings and poignant mishaps. It's unspeakably awful. Please don't watch it. The film reminds me of the Israel I grew up regularly visiting from the early 80s onwards. It was a country of congealing institutional buffets, turgid gravel-voiced balladeers on the radio, the smell of cockroach spray, half-built apartment blocks and awkward TV programmes filmed on shaky sets.

I loved my childhood Israel.

Israel seemed to be a work in progress. Life was alien and extraordinary in many respects, and I was awed by scruffy kids in army uniforms casually toting rifles, but its deep mediocrity in the stuff of everyday life meant the country also felt *comfortable*. This wasn't a place of intimidating excellence, but a country whose citizens phlegmatically accepted external threats and the need for military service, while going back to enjoy their terrible music, awful TV and lousy food in tatty apartments.

On my last visit to Israel I enjoyed world-class food in Tel Aviv, admired the skyscrapers lining the Ayalon freeway, observed the well-dressed young people toting the latest smartphones and was whisked to the airport via the up-to-date rail system. It left me cold. This Israel was dynamic and brilliant, living at the cutting edge that was also an existential knife edge. Yafit Gimmel and the mediocre Israeliness she represented is passing into history. Her daughter-in-law, who inherited Gimmel's role as chief Israeli advertising shill, is slicker and lacks her mother-in-law's haggard features. I fear that, sooner or later, the brilliant start-up nation will produce an AI-powered cyborg shill to replace Israel's human hucksters forever, and the Israeli products they tout will be high quality and worth buying.

That Israel's cultural output has reached new heights of achievement during a time of growing political hopelessness, suggests that the presence of liberally minded and adventurous cultural production cannot in itself triumph over reactionary political trends. That doesn't mean that culture – in Israel or anywhere else – is worthless without justice, but it does suggest that, whatever perspective you take on Israel, excellence provides neither a case for or against the existence of the state.

For those who see themselves as having progressive values and also believe in at least the principle of a Jewish state in Israel, the erosion of Israeli mediocrity should be of greater concern than the Israeli cultural vibrancy they often cling to and take pride in. Israeli mediocrity was spawned by a state still in development, with all kinds of possibilities still on the table. It is easier to find a place in an everyday culture that is rough around the edges than in an extraordinary state. Everyday mediocrity provides a kind of unnoticed baseline for a common culture in a fractured state. Arab citizens of Israel, strictly orthodox Jews and secular Tel Avivians all share in the shoddiness of Osem's bounty; or at least they once did. In an Israel with world-class pop-up restaurants, boutique wineries and small-batch olive oil producers, where is the common culture?

A common everyday culture may at least make the possibility of coexistence more thinkable; humans may connect better with each other when they share down-to-earth tastes and everyday experiences. Maybe BDS activists are correct, albeit not in the way they might think: Even the most trivial products can help to normalise Israel yet they also normalise the possibility of a common experience of everyday life, and in that sense, the mediocre likes of Bamba may be more subversive than people think. Even if the huge imbalance between the Israeli and Palestinian economies means that Israeli products do not circulate on an even playing field, tastelessness knows no boundaries.

Building peace, one snack at a time
Right now, the possibility of Israelis and Palestinians joining hands in celebration of cheap snacks is further away than ever. They remain locked into the logic of the extraordinary.

Palestinians, to the extent they are able to, take pride in the beauty of their land, their poets and their olive oil. In mourning the disaster in Gaza there is often talk of the writers, universities and historic sites that were turned to ashes. No one mourns the mediocre hummus restaurants, the incompetent teachers, the dull bores who were consumed in the same inferno. Those who struggle for Palestine see no benefit to eulogising lost banality; they make extraordinary efforts to justify the saving of an extraordinary people from an extraordinary enemy. This is what the attention economy desires. It also sends a dangerous message: that the existence of Palestinians, Israelis, Jews or any other people is conditional on them being interesting and 'worth' saving.

The more that Palestine is treated as extraordinary, the greater the likelihood of ultimate disappointment. Even if Palestine did turn into whatever the many different factions among pro-Palestinian activists wish it to be – an egalitarian secular state called Palestine where all its citizens live in harmony, an Islamist theocracy from which Jews are expelled, an extension of Russian or Iranian empire, or maybe just a Palestinian state alongside the Jewish state – it would still be a massive disappointment. It's precisely because the coalition for Palestine is so broad that the success of any one of the many visions of what Palestine should be would inevitably be a letdown to at least part of that coalition.

Today it's in few people's interest to point to the contradictory motivations of those who seek justice for Palestinians. There's no chance of any final victory in the near future and, given the desperate situation Palestinians find themselves in right now, why open that can of worms? Even the fissure between Fatah and Hamas is, at times of existential crisis, smoothed over to a degree. For those,

Jews and otherwise, who oppose all or some visions of what Palestine could be, there is a tendency to lump everyone who struggles for Palestinian together in an undifferentiated mass, defined by its more dubious elements. Those who accuse Western pro-Palestinian demonstrators of being either useful idiots for or supporters of Hamas and who ignore the heterogeneity of the movement, are sometimes confirmed in their view by activists who insist on unity and solidarity.

If and when Palestinians manage to achieve a solution to their plight, this mutual tendency to ignore the diversity within Palestine and among its global supporters will likely become impossible. Then again, there is a long history of overseas supporters losing interest once the national liberation struggles they support are won. Vietnam, South Africa, East Timor, Algeria ... they are all on their own now.

Right now, the eyes of the world are on Palestine; or at least that's what it looks like. 'Palestine' is sometimes something other than Palestine. The cause is often tied into a great range of other causes. I was struck by an online advert I saw in 2024 for a meeting for Earth Day organised by the US progressive activist organisation Code Pink, which proclaimed, 'We cannot end climate change without ending the genocide in Gaza.'[8] Connecting Palestinian liberation with action against climate change has become common. Another example is a campaign group in the UK called Fossil Free Books, set up within the book trade, to campaign on two issues: climate change and Palestine.[9] In addition to climate change, the cause of Palestine is, variously, the chosen cause of anti-racism, queer liberation and any other liberation struggle. It has become foundational to a vast range of other causes.

Any solution to Israel–Palestine will not stop climate change, endemic racism and the woes of the world. Even the most utopian solution to Israel–Palestine might be greeted ecstatically but the next morning everyone will wake up to the same burning world. Liberated Palestinians will never be able to repay their debt to their supporters. How could they? How could anybody? The investment in hope and passion in their cause is so great that no political or military solution can ever hope to repay it.

Settling for mundanity

I don't know what the solution is or even if there is one beyond more death and destruction. I do know that settling for the quiet dissatisfactions of everyday life is part of the solution. True liberation and true peace will be found in dull insignificance. That is an enormous challenge to achieve, but there are precedents.

While writing this chapter I realised something: I didn't know the names of any of Northern Ireland's current political leaders. I only remembered Jeffrey Donaldson, who had been obliged to relinquish leadership of the Democratic Unionist Party after being charged with historic sexual offenses. There was a time, though, when Northern Irish politicians were virtually household names in the UK; Gerry Adams, Martin McGuinness, David Trimble, Ian Paisley and John Hume were all big news as Northern Ireland slowly moved towards ending the Troubles in the 1990s. Political geeks like me would know others too, smaller party leaders like John Alderdice, Gary McMichael and David Ervine. During the Troubles we'd also hear about the alphabet soup of Loyalist and Republican militia, the big ones like the IRA and the UVF, as well as smaller ones like the INLA and LVF. For a territory of fewer than 2 million people, the degree of focus on Northern Ireland was far in excess of its size and geopolitical significance.

It's not that Northern Ireland is 'solved'. Aside from the continuing presence of militia groups, the Brexit process has, and continues to be, entangled in the delicate politics of the territory and a peace process dependent on an open border with the Irish Republic. Yet Northern Ireland today lacks the bloodiness of the past. It's easier to ignore and its politicians have turned into regional politicians, rather than figures who attract national and global attention. The territory is slowly becoming a small part of the world, with significant local problems that occasionally lead to national problems; no more than that.

At some point in the peace process, Northern Irish political leaders, as well as the militia some of them were allied with, had to find a way to accept that, if the process was successful, they would no longer be important. There would be no more trips to the White House and no more Nobel Prizes; no more terrorist 'spectaculars' filling the front pages. Somehow they managed to accept this, and that acceptance played an important role in making the conflict manageable.

Of course, bad things do happen in darkness. Total obscurity is as dangerous as universal attention. Western Saharans and Sri Lankan Tamils, to give two examples, know what it is to be ignored. Perhaps the key in Northern Ireland was that there was 'just enough' attention that it spurred world leaders to try to address it, without the whole world jumping in. In any case, can Israeli and Palestinian leaders manage to accept some version of Northern Irish obscurity?

No, they can't. Not yet, anyway.

Aside from the fact that Israel–Palestine is a far more lethal, far more asymmetric conflict, as well as a destabilising force in the Middle East as a whole, too many people *care* about what happens there. The precondition for Northern Ireland becoming less significant was that, while there was and is global interest in the conflict, it was never as broad and as fervent as interest in Israel–Palestine has been. On the far left, it was treated as one part of a grab-bag of liberation struggles around the world, not *the* struggle. While Irish republicans in the US were important in raising money and sometimes political support for the IRA, this was not an issue that 'everyone' had to have a view on. There were no pro-IRA demonstrations in Paraguay and no pro-loyalist sit-ins in Fiji.

When it comes to Israel–Palestine, there's no escaping the global spotlight. We are not even close to a situation where politicians and fighters can retire into obscurity. Populists like Benjamin Netanyahu can bask in their global importance. IDF spokespeople can develop huge followings on Instagram. Yasser Arafat never had to contemplate the prospect of being the leader of a small and insignificant state with no oil and rampant social problems. And if the spotlight fails to shine on you for too long, you can always do as Hamas' Yahya Sinwar did, and perpetrate an atrocity that puts you back in the limelight.

Then there's people like me. I'm neither Israel nor Palestine. But just by being a Diaspora Jew with a modest public profile I get the occasional sprinkling of magic fairy dust through my association with the The Biggest Issue in The World. I am Important too; so are we all, Jews and Palestinians. It doesn't matter what my actual views are; someone will want to love-bomb me for holding them – or conduct a more literal bombing.

No more.

It's time to become an everyday Jew, an ordinary Jew, a normal Jew, a boring Jew.

Can I even imagine what that might look like?

Chapter Ten

Sacred smallness

The golden age

One of the themes in post-7 October Diaspora Jewish discourse has been an elegy for a Jewishness that is passing into history. The most striking example was Franklin Foer's essay 'The Golden Age of American Jews Is Ending', published in *The Atlantic* in March 2024.[1] Foer rhapsodised about post-war American Jewish culture:

> As anti-Semitism faded, American Jewish civilization exploded in a rush of creativity. For a time, the great Jewish novel—books by Saul Bellow, Philip Roth, Norman Mailer, Joseph Heller, and Bernard Malamud, inflected with Yiddish and references to pickled herring—was the great American novel. Under the influence of Lenny Bruce, Sid Caesar, Mel Brooks, Elaine May, Gilda Radner, Woody Allen, and many others, American comedy appropriated the Jewish joke, and the ironic sensibility contained within, as its own.

Foer argued that this golden age is ending, as the liberal society in which it flourished is assaulted by illiberal antisemitism on the left and right:

> The forces arrayed against Jews, on the right and the left, are far more powerful than they were 50 years ago.

The surge of anti-Semitism is a symptom of the decay of democratic habits, a leading indicator of rising authoritarianism. When anti-Semitism takes hold, conspiracy theory hardens into conventional wisdom, embedding violence in thought and then in deadly action. A society that holds its Jews at arm's length is likely to be more intent on hunting down scapegoats than addressing underlying defects. Although it is hardly an iron law of history, such societies are prone to decline. England entered a long dark age after expelling its Jews in 1290. Czarist Russia limped toward revolution after the pogroms of the 1880s. If America persists on its current course, it would be the end of the Golden Age not just for the Jews, but for the country that nurtured them.

Regardless of whether Foer's threat assessment is correct or not, any 'golden age' will end at some point. If the American Jewish golden age depended on the persistence of a particular kind of (liberal) political system, then by definition it was built on complacency, since all political systems are transitory. Foer seems to go even further, suggesting that a Jewish golden age is the precondition of a wider golden age. Are we really that important?

In any case, the American Jewish golden age may not have been as golden as it appeared. Yes, Jewish culture made an enormous impact on post-war American culture and society; but what kind of culture? A culture of performative angst and wit, of public excellence and insouciance; above all, a culture of intense, even solipsistic interest in Jewish being. It was a culture that de-emphasised doing Jewish and the hard work of maintaining community. It was a culture in which Jewish communities and the organisations that served them struggled to retain affiliation and activity. It was a culture of public visibility and private ossification, marked by ever-desperate attempts by communal organisations to get Jews to do something Jewish.

There is a certain Jewish pride in pointing out how we have survived while other civilisations rose and fell. Benjamin Disraeli drew on some of this pride in his well-known riposte to an antisemitic comment in the House of Commons: 'Yes, I am a Jew, and while the ancestors of the right honourable gentleman were brutal savages in an unknown island, mine were priests in the temple of Solomon.' Yet the temple of Solomon was ultimately destroyed by the Babylonians and its successor was destroyed by the Romans. That the Romans didn't survive doesn't change the fact that Jews mourn the destruction of the Temple to this day. The lesson of history should surely be to keep a sceptical attitude during a particular golden age and not to drink the civilisational Kool-Aid. Even if there have been times when we made a sizeable impact on the world, nothing comes for free.

In his celebrated book of the same name, Yuri Slezkine argued that the twentieth century was 'The Jewish Century'.[2] What he meant was that the 'Mercurian' skills through which Jews had survived as a minority Diaspora people – mobility, translation, service provision rather than production, wit and knowledge – became the pre-eminent skills that survival in modernity required. Slezkine's argument might seem celebratory but, as he argues in the case of Russian Jewry, in the end the Mercurian nature of the Jewish people did not save it from unprecedented punishment. The Jewish people may sometimes be the embodiment of the zeitgeist; that doesn't mean we always benefit from it.

What we are seeing from many Jewish leaders and organisations today is a paradoxical strategy that bemoans the declining status of Jewry in the US and elsewhere while at the same mobilising 'golden age' practices of influence. We are witnessing ever-more desperate attempts to make ourselves bigger, prouder, more assertive and more public.

One example is JewBelong, an American organisation whose aim is 'Supporting Joyous Judaism and Confronting Antisemitism'.[3] They are best known for placing eye-catching billboards in prominent locations, bearing messages such as 'We're just 75 years from the gas chambers. So no, a billboard calling out Jewish hate isn't an overreaction.' As they explain on their website:

> These days, antisemitism is growing, and well, it can be hard to be a Joyous Jew when there's a target on your back. That's why we're raising awareness about the problem! JewBelong's brave approach calls out Jew-hate. Our signature pink and white billboards, billboard trucks, website, and strong social media presence powerfully confront antisemitism as well as support Joyous Judaism. This loud and proud message is starting important conversations, creating excitement in the Jewish community, and garnering mainstream media attention!

This approach, of fighting antisemitism through public prominence, has proved very appealing. In the UK, the Campaign Against Antisemitism (CAA) has followed a similar approach, including using billboards and getting as much media coverage as possible. A CAA newsletter from March 2024 was headed 'Making antisemitism frontpage news', implying an axiomatic belief in the power of publicity.[4]

In November 2024, the CAA organised a 'National March Against Antisemitism' through central London. Photos from the day show the front row of the demonstration dominated by prominent Jewish and non-Jewish celebrities, most notably the actress Tracy-Ann Oberman and the TV presenter Rachel Riley, with only the Chief Rabbi and the head of the CAA to make up the numbers.[5] Another British Jewish celebrity, the writer and comedian David Baddiel, has become a high-profile fighter of antisemitism. His 2021 book *Jews Don't Count* became a bestseller in the UK, also attracting attention in the US.[6] The following year he presented a documentary with the same name, featuring other celebrity Jews such as David Schwimmer and Sarah Silverman, as well as famous writers such as Neil Gaiman and Howard Jacobson.

The involvement of high-profile Jewish public figures in the fight against antisemitism has certainly propelled the issue onto the public agenda. This way of fighting antisemitism follows the 'golden age' blueprint. Authority to speak on antisemitism is tacitly granted (or contested, by other kinds of Jews) on the basis of one's profile outside the Jewish community. The risk is that this prioritisation of the famous will reproduce the golden age's neglect of Jewish everyday doing.

Perhaps the desire to go public reflects traumatic folk memories of quietist Jewish populations who feared attention and sought to make themselves discreet and uncomplaining. That didn't always work. Such memories are particularly important in certain kinds of Jewish left politics today. Those who claim to be heirs to the anti-Zionist political tradition celebrate their ancestors' aggressive anti-fascism and resistance before and during the Holocaust. Today's Zionists also laud their ancestors' resistance too. The supposed 'meekness' of those Jews who did not resist acts as a reproach to Jews who would avoid today's public sphere.

Vision conquest

Of course, going public is not the only Jewish strategy. As I mentioned in Chapter Six, the aftermath of the 7 October attacks saw a wave of institutional responses. These included attempts at developing coherent policies for how Jews could get through what was widely seen as a crisis. For many Jewish leaders, a crisis needed not just organisation, but a plan and a vision.

There is no shortage of visions of what the Jewish people should be. One recent example is the collection *Jewish Priorities: Sixty-five Proposals for the Future of Our People*, edited by David Hazony and published at the start of 2024.[7] Describing itself as 'an unprecedented snapshot of a generation of Jews', the breadth of contributors is broader than one usually finds in such exercises, Haredi and secular, left and right, and so on. It includes everything from Dara Horn criticising how Holocaust education is carried out to Natan Sharansky arguing for an even more public form of it. While a sometimes bracing read, the one assumption that remains largely unquestioned is that the project itself is, in some way, 'good for the Jews'. While I certainly don't see it as 'bad for the Jews', I do see it as symptomatic of an obsession with defining, guiding, criticising and inspiring what Jews should be doing. Given that the plurality of these visions tends to cancel each other out, Jews create visions for the Jewish people in the knowledge that they are only one among many and, therefore, they can only guide one segment of the Jewish people.

Shaul Magid, a renowned Jewish American scholar, contributed a defence of a Diasporic Jewish culture to *Jewish Priorities*. This is part of his larger non-Zionist project to envision the Jewish people as 'exilic', as outlined in his 2023 book *The Necessity of Exile*.[8] In that book, he argued that the liberal Zionist dream – normative across 'mainstream' Jewry in the US,

UK and many other countries – has now been superseded by the illiberal reality of Israel.⁹ Yet what, in the end, is Magid's own contribution? He offers yet another vision to add to the pile, to be discussed and to be fought over.

This desire to shape the Jewish future distances us from the pragmatics of everyday life. It may be an extraordinary thing for a confirmed intellectual to say, but Jews may need to start questioning what the life of the mind can do for us. Or at least we might start to question what the Jewish mind should be considering. As I pointed out in Chapter Four, systematic attempts to understand what Jewish people are doing now, as opposed to envisioning what they should be doing now, are often conspicuous by their absence. The relatively low priority given in most Jewish populations to learning from everyday practice also means we sometimes ignore sources of emerging hope. Entrenched divisions between Jews may be insoluble in theory but can be manageable in practice. For instance, I know from my own modest experience with the Haredi Jewish community in London that what might appear in public to be bulwarks against relationships, coexist with pragmatism, quiet discussions and even friendship. Another example is campus relationships between Jews, Muslims and pro-Palestinian activists. These days the divides may seem unbridgeable, but as the ethnographer Ruth Sheldon has shown in the UK, when students are able to engage in confidential dialogue groups out of the public eye, better relationships can and are built.¹⁰

Given the intense Jewish interest in vision, there is always a danger that Jewish initiatives can be 'oversold', creating expectations that are difficult to fulfill. In spring 2023 a merger process was announced between the separate Reform and Liberal movements in the UK. The proposed merger was widely welcomed, including by me. Merging two closely related movements enables greater efficiency, greater market share and better use of resources. As the process has unfolded, one of the most notable aspects of it has been the evident desire to be much more than a pragmatic exercise. For example, the 2023 joint Rosh Hashanah message from Rabbi Josh Levy, CEO of Reform Judaism, and Rabbi Charley Baginsky, CEO of Liberal Judaism, proclaimed:

> We need you to help us develop the vision; to help us imagine what a shared, sustainable and effective movement will look like. To help us think through how we have a more powerful voice in the Jewish, faith and national spheres, how we invest in what makes Jewish life flourish, how we recognise the centrality of our synagogues and communities and support their development, and how we ensure that we have growth and breadth for the future.[11]

The assumption that 'we' need to 'build' a vision seems to be taken for granted. This is how Jewish organisational change is sold to funders and stakeholders. Yet why does there need to be a vision beyond what is already being done by Reform and Liberal Jews in their synagogues and within the wider Jewish community? Why is that not 'enough'? Why can't Jews sometimes change things for dull reasons?

It seems to me that Jews are on a kind of hamster wheel. We have to continually come up with reasons to do things, with visions of how things should be, with plans that guide how our communities should develop. There has to be a story, a narrative. Jewish tradition is suffused with such narratives. The ark of history must bend towards a Jewish end, the messianic age, whose nature and imminence we may profoundly disagree with each other about, but whose deep narrative structure we cleave to.

What if there was no destiny or purpose? What if Jewish life were just the sum total of Jews doing things as Jews? Theologically that may be anathema, at least officially. Yet even the most messianically focused sects within Haredi Judaism have so much Jewish stuff to do that it is unlikely that the ultimate purpose of it all is born in mind every minute of every hour of every day. The everyday practice of Judaism, in whatever form, is experienced in a succession of moments in which destiny disappears into the now.

Progressive Jewish overreach

In the last few years, a particular song has become wildly popular in many Jewish milieux. Its chorus proclaims:

> I have a voice, my voice is powerful, my voice can change the world

The final verse doubles down:

> I will fight for the truth, I'll stand up for what's right, I will use this strength I've been given
>   And be a light ...

'I Have a Voice' by the American 'composer, multi-instrumentalist and prayer leader' Elana Arian is sweet and empowering. We all need to hear sometimes that we matter, that the world we are born into isn't totally outside our control. On the other hand, in an age of online performativity, when everyone potentially has a public voice in any society with at least a modicum of freedom, Arian's lyric creates expectations that are hard to realise. Voices are ubiquitous, but some are more powerful than others. The idea that changing the world is a matter of using our voices can be excessively optimistic.

The popularity of 'I Have a Voice' in Jewish summer camps and conferences demonstrates how speaking out in order to change the world has become a widely shared Jewish goal. Arian's song also demonstrates how this value is often only shakily embedded in religious tradition. The only Hebrew in the song is the blessing for God 'making me in God's image', which is pretty essential theologically but not a specific injunction to speak out and change the world. While some other theologies whose desire to change the world is grounded on a deeper and broader engagement with Jewish textual tradition, it is as much contemporary histories and traditions that are compelling many Jews today to go out and try to change the world, successfully or otherwise.

The process of Jewish emancipation that began in the eighteenth century, while variable and inconsistent, created the possibility for Jews to intervene politically in the world in ways barely imagined by their ancestors. That opportunity was part of wider processes of democratisation and citizenship that enabled mass movements, political parties and other ways in which those previously excluded in the political life of the nation could make their voices heard. Sometimes Jewish voices did change the world. Benjamin Disraeli, Karl Marx, Rosa Luxemburg and countless others offer inspiration to today's Jews. Key moments such as the Battle of Cable Street, the Warsaw ghetto uprising and Rabbi Joshua Heschel marching at Selma with Martin Luther King have become part of the Jewish pantheon. Jews have made pivotal contributions to left-wing, liberal and, more recently, right-wing politics. Whether you want to raise your voice to preserve the rainforests or to burn them down, to stand with African-Americans or set the cops on them, to liberate the working class or the billionaire class, there's a Jewish story to inspire you.

All these precedents for Jewish activism have raised the possibility that *the world needs us*. This desire to be part of the Jewish contribution to the world has even infiltrated what were once highly insular forms of Jewish politics. While there have always been forms of Zionism that saw themselves as part of a universal politics, there has also been a strong strain within the movement and the state it formed that sought nothing more than a place to be securely Jewish in a hostile world. Today, while left Zionism struggles to remain part of global progressive politics, there are multiple opportunities for right-leaning Zionists to be part of globalised conservative movements and to position themselves as a vanguard in a global struggle for 'Western' civilisation. It is only the Haredi Jewish world that largely eschews positioning themselves as part of a broader, values-driven political struggle, although even here, in local politics in particular, public representatives of the community sometimes make the right noises about common values.

Does the world really need us? I hope not. Because the world would be doomed if it did. There just aren't enough of us. Even if every Jew everywhere were to dedicate their lives to activism, we are a few million of billions. We aren't everywhere either; Jew-free Burkina Faso and Vanuatu are somehow going to have to manage on their own.

I am being a little unfair. Only in the most orthodox forms of Judaism do Jews have such a unique role as the chosen ones who will bring about the redemption of the entire world once the messiah comes. Still, there is more than a hint of claiming an outsize role in the world in contemporary progressive Jewish activism. The kabbalistic concept of *tikkun olam* ('repair of the world') refers to the redemption that comes from bringing together the shattered vessels of holiness in the world. In recent decades, though, a tradition has grown up, particularly within progressive Judaisms, that treats *tikkun olam* as an ethical practice of good deeds and social activism. While the redemption that such acts are designed to bring about is often vaguely defined and most tikkun olamists would be at pains to say that Jews are not the only ones who can play their part in this process, it's hard to avoid a certain grandiloquence.

Secular left forms of Jewish activism can also be swept up in an overestimation of how important we are. Although orthodox Marxism doesn't have the hold on Jewish radicals as it once did, the hope of true communism has messianic resonances. Many Jews continue to find in radical causes something that is not just politically justifiable, but also *Jewishly* justifiable. Jewish Voice for Peace, the US movement that is best known for its anti-Zionism, grounds itself in a specifically Jewish history:

> Like generations of Jewish leftists before us, we fight for the liberation of all people. We believe that through organizing, we can and will dismantle the institutions and structures that sustain injustice and grow something new, joyful, beautiful, and life-sustaining in their place ...[12]

Secular or religious, radical, liberal or conservative, the modern Jewish activist tradition is not just deeply embedded in many of the streams that make up today's Jewish people, it has also become *essentialised*. By this I mean that particular forms of activism are seen as an intrinsic and eternal part of what it is to be a Jew. For example, Tzelem, a British coalition of rabbis which aims 'to organise Jewish clerical voices on social and economic justice issues in the UK' takes its name from 'the Jewish principle that we are all created *b'tzelem Elokim* – in the image of G-d [sic].'[13] Among its principles is the following:

> We respond to the divine command to create a civil society in the UK that exemplifies our beliefs and values as Jews, as demanded by the mitzvot, our prophets, our ancestral rabbis/teachers, and our texts. Our Torah demands that we engage with and care about our wider society and matters of justice that affect the vulnerable in our society.[14]

The use of 'demands' is striking here. To strive for social justice in the UK is not just a Jewish 'add-on', it is a commandment that Jews cannot shirk. The implication is that this struggle is and has always been the essence of Judaism.

Of course, politically conservative Jews may sneer at such 'woke' forms of Judaism and what they might see as textual cherry-picking to justify contemporary mores.[15] Yet right-wing politics is even more bound to notions of essentialism, just different ones. In terms of grounding a world view, there is no difference between asserting the eternity of fixed gender roles, for example, and the eternity of struggle for justice for the oppressed. It's not so surprising that conservative forms of Judaism argue that there is a right and a wrong way to be and do Jewish; it is more surprising when progressives do the same.

For most of history Jews were in no position to do good for anyone but themselves, and sometimes not even that. Some of the most commonly cited sources for social-justice-minded Judaism could only be enacted during the brief periods in which a sovereign Jewish state existed. The much-quoted commandment in Exodus (22:20) 'Do not oppress

the stranger for you were strangers in Egypt' is predicated
on having sufficient power to oppress the stranger in the first
place. While more liberal Jews may not be uncomfortable, at
least in principle, with Zionism and other means by which
modern Jews have sought power in the world, it is far more
difficult for Jews who reject Zionism to acknowledge how
elements of the Jewish social justice tradition are based on
the possibility of a Jewish state.

'Radical' visions of what it means to be Jewish are therefore
not immune to reductive narrowness. At the 'Emergency Seder'
held in April 2024 in New York, the author and activist Naomi
Klein delivered a stirring speech denouncing Zionism as a 'false
idol' that was 'profaning' Jewish tradition:

> It is a false idol that takes our most profound biblical sto-
> ries of justice and emancipation from slavery – the story
> of Passover itself – and turns them into brutalist weapons
> of colonial land theft, roadmaps for ethnic cleansing and
> genocide.
>
> It is a false idol that has taken the transcendent idea of
> the promised land – a metaphor for human liberation that
> has traveled across multiple faiths to every corner of this
> globe – and dared to turn it into a deed of sale for a milita-
> ristic ethnostate.
>
> It is a false idol that has led far too many of our own
> people down a deeply immoral path that now has them jus-
> tifying the shredding of core commandments: thou shalt not
> kill. Thou shalt not steal. Thou shalt not covet.
>
> Zionism is a false idol that has betrayed every Jewish
> value, including the value we place on questioning – a prac-
> tice embedded in the Seder with its four questions asked by
> the youngest child.[16]

While I am a Jew who believes that Zionism is neither sacrosanct nor eternally valid, this speech worried me immensely. To embrace essentialism in opposing Zionism is to simply take the boundaries that other Jews have erected against people like Klein and flip them for your own benefit. There is nothing radical about dividing humanity into the pure and the impure.

One of the most popular slogans in US protests against the Gaza war has been 'No one is free until everybody's free' (originally coined by the African-American civil-rights activist Fannie Lou Hamer in 1971).[17] For Jews horrified by Israel's actions, the slogan can resonate as a defiant insistence that Jewish safety and security cannot be bought at the expense of others. The slogan can also imply a refusal to accept 'normal' life and to insist on a state of emergency. At times, the slogan can take on a distinctly menacing undertone. During the campus occupation in Columbia University in May 2024, the university's chapter of the National Lawyers Guild sent a defiant message of resistance that included the lines:

> Our safety cannot be predicated on the oppression of others, whether campus protestors or Palestinians. No Jew is safe until everyone is safe, and no Jew is free until Palestine is free.[18]

If 'no one is free till everyone is free', normal life can only be a delusion. Those who have privilege – and Jews are sometimes treated as privilege incarnate on the left – can only be moral if they struggle endlessly for the freedom of others.

I agree that there is something obscene in getting too comfortable in such a broken world, particularly when that comfort is achieved on the backs of the suffering and oppressed.

But don't we also deserve the odd weekend off? No one can be 'on' all the time.

Today's Jewish radicals may have created viable models of political action, but they have rarely thought about what everyday Jewish life might look like outside the struggle. There is sometimes more than a hint of self-flagellation, a conviction that Jews cannot be allowed to have anything for themselves alone. Prior to Pesach in 2024, Joseph Finlay, a British-Jewish writer and musician with a long history of anti-Zionist activism, published an essay taking issue with a call for Jewish families to set an empty place for one of the missing Israeli hostages in Gaza. While Finlay was not dismissive of Jewish concern for the hostages, Pesach could not simply be about us:

> Just as the future messianic promise of return has been turned into a real-life state-building project, seder rituals concerned with the intangible future have become literalised, to focus attention on very real hostages. The ideal has been sacrificed in service of the political. I think we need to be concerned about this. It is part of the shrinking of Judaism, from a religion with universal themes and concern for humanity in general, to a narrow peoplehood cult, in which the losses and gains of our ethno-cultural group are the only things that count. The liberation of the Israelites from Egyptian slavery should not be read narrowly and paralleled only with the imprisonment or freedom of contemporary Jews. Our Passovers need to be concerned with all instances of slavery and celebrate all who have gained their rights, looking forward to a messianic era when all are liberated. The campaign to place pictures of hostages is part of the ongoing project to nationalise Judaism, to interpret 'let my people' go as 'set free all captive Israelis and Jews'.

Of course, I hope that the hostages are released, immediately. But we need to hope for more than that.[19]

While Joseph Finlay is deeply embedded in Jewish life beyond the radical Jewish left, his essay seemed to show a deliberate ignorance of how seders actually work. Yes, the seder is a repository of stories, theologies and liturgies of extraordinary depth and richness. The seder is also about an aged relative spilling wine on the tablecloth, bored kids asking when we will eat, airing of much-loved melodies and my mother's macaroons. Finlay's vision of Pesach is so significant that it paradoxically becomes empty, reduced to an 'author's message'.

As someone who is not too far away from Joseph Finlay politically, I *should* be getting my ideological rocks off to liberationist seders. In reality, I can't stop myself mangling the phrase from the 60s, 'if I can't have supper quizzes I don't want to be part of your revolution.' The Jewish left have a very long way to go in this regard; the stolid politics of 'mainstream' Jewry may sometimes frustrate me, but no tradition survives without the mundane. By its very nature, a constant state of emergency in which 'no one is free till we are all free' only works for those who are into activism. Outside that cohort, most will not choose to live in that permanent state of emergency unless compelled. Maybe when the climate crisis reaches its height that will happen. Until then, while everyday life is still an option for Jews, most will take that option with occasional excursions into self-righteousness.

The reductiveness of making Jewish life synonymous with getting out into the world and trying to change it offers a dubious strategy for long-term Jewish survival. Of course, one argument that is often made about Israel, particularly on the left but not exclusively, is that our *moral* survival is at stake.

The problem is that such arguments depend on essentialist views of what Jews' true moral destiny consists of, and these ultimately come down to banal assertion. Are Jews a people of extraordinary moral insight or a people who are irredeemably tarnished? The answer, of course, is yes. What Jews and others disagree on is which Jews fall into which category. So what seems like an urgent existential question is really a question with an utterly dull and predictable answer. We are morally all over the place and are likely to always be so. Even if one particular moral essentialism is 'correct', there will always be others. Either the morally pure and the morally corrupted Jews survive together or neither will.

There is a constant risk of hubris when Jews put themselves at the heart of the human story. Can Jews whose Jewish lives consist of a weary succession of petitions, demonstrations, vigils and ceremonies avoid burnout and disillusionment? Would it really be so wrong if our Jewish lives also allowed us to seek temporary refuge in ultimately trivial activities as we recuperated from wider struggles?

It's time to think the unthinkable: Making ourselves *smaller*.

Tzimtzum

In April 2024, Michelle Rosenberg, an editor at London's *Jewish News*, reported back from a trip to Israel organised by the UK charity the United Jewish Israel Appeal. The trip made a profound impact on her, and she concluded:

> Having felt so liberated, so viscerally proud of my culture, my history, my heritage, the thought of coming back to the UK and having to re-shrink that identity, to hide myself away for my own safety, to worry about my youngest daughter wearing her Israel tour hoodie or my eldest

wearing her great-grandmother's Magen David necklace, was profoundly disturbing.

I realised, as Jews in the UK, how much we have normalised making ourselves smaller.[20]

'Smallness', as Rosenberg understands it, is a bleak, even shameful condition. She continues a long tradition of contrasting the meekness of Diaspora Jewish existence with the fullness and pride of Jewish life in a Jewish state. Jews in the Diaspora, particularly those living in the centuries before the establishment of the state of Israel, have often needed to practise discretion, shrinking from the inevitable blow that sooner or later always arrived. Whether or not Rosenberg's take on the state of the Jewish people in the UK in 2024 was based on a proportionate risk assessment is irrelevant; the idea that small is not beautiful is deeply embedded in Jewish culture.

Jewishly, I am no shrinking violet. This is my sixth book on Jewish issues and I never miss a chance to preach to the world about Jewish affairs. But when I read Rosenberg's article it kind of flicked a switch in my brain: 'Smallness, eh? That sounds really appealing right now.' In fact, it always has appealed to me to some extent. Even when, in my younger days, I felt sad as the plane left Ben Gurion Airport, taking me back to rainy London, I nonetheless felt an almost physical relief to step out of the plane at Heathrow. There I was in the eye of the storm; here I am no one. There, by virtue of being a Jew in Israel, I was part of a unique experiment; here, I am barely a part of our island story.

Of course, I have the luxury of being able to choose smallness. I don't wear a *kippah* or a Star of David. Even so, there have been times when I have hidden aspects of my Jewishness. When I was learning Hebrew, for example, I made a conscious decision not to take my textbook on public transport. Still, that's part of a wider desire not to be noticed when I don't want to be noticed, and I rarely wear metal T-shirts in public either.

Not everyone is like me, though, and I would fight for the right for Jews to be as visible as they wish. Enforced smallness is oppression. *Choosing* smallness, though, may have a value that Jews dismiss prematurely. After all, when God created the universe, God had to become smaller too ...

The concept of *tzimtzum*, developed by the sixteenth-century kabbalist Isaac Luria, is an elegant way of managing an apparent paradox: How could the boundless infinity of the divine create something as finite as life? Luria's answer is that God's first act of creation was to *tzimtzum* ('contract') God's infinite light in order to make space for the finite realm of existence. This also helps us understand questions of free will; human beings are part of that space that is at once divine and outside of the infinite light.

I don't think Isaac Luria would be particularly impressed by my taking *tzimtzum* out of the realm of mystic paradox; I am nonetheless going to do it. *Tzimtzum* provides a useful tool in thinking about Jews' place in the world and in particular how we might offer an alternative to the excesses of Jewification. Maybe it is true that Jewish life and tradition can potentially encompass the world and everything in it, but Jewish life and tradition became possible in the first place within one small corner of the world. While Jews involve themselves publicly in the world out of a refusal to be cowed, Jewish life and tradition require that we also attend sometimes to our own small Jewish world.

Even if you believe that Jewish life and tradition is extraordinary and extraordinarily important, sometimes it's worth pretending we are just a small and irrelevant people. Everyone needs to take a day off now and again.

The good news is that Jews do, in fact, know how to *tzimtzum*. As I have shown in this book, Jewish life is full of trivial everydayness. For many Jews, Jewish life *is small already*. The problem is that 'public' Jews tend to emphasise the big stuff. We need a language in which we can speak of our smallness without shame, a language that can help contract us.

Chapter Eleven

A small-minded people

In praise of parochialism

When I was growing up in 1970s and 80s Britain, the British Jewish community was often described by its critics as small-minded, inward-looking, parochial and insular. It never occurred to me to think that these could be anything but bad things. As an eighteen-year-old in 1989, I devoured Stephen Brook's book *The Club: The Jews of Modern Britain*, which was wonderfully scabrous in his indictment of the dullness of the community:

> philistinism and intolerance within the fold have persuaded countless gifted Jews to direct their energies away from the community; and British Jews loyal to their religious and cultural tradition have always sought to adopt the lowest possible profile. It is certainly respectable to be Jewish in Britain, but it's neither exciting nor chic.[1]

I knew this wasn't entirely fair and that there were pockets of vibrancy in British Jewry. Still, I yearned for a community that would be dynamic, outward-facing and unabashedly Jewish. To my surprise, in the 1990s and 2000s, a more dynamic community did emerge, based on the efforts of Jewish leaders and communal activists who agreed with critiques like Brook's. At university in the early 1990s, I was repelled by the boring and insular Jewish society and felt sure that there was no place for me in British Jewry going forward. In barely a decade I found myself engaged to be married to a Reform rabbi, whom I'd met through Limmud, the learning conference whose dramatic growth in the 1990s exemplified the new dynamism. I had also been mentored into contributing to the process of policy-oriented research which played an important part in the transformation of the community.

Today, though, I wonder whether the insular and dull community I grew up in was so bad after all. At the very least, it *belonged to us*. Most people were not very interested in British Jews; even if Israel was rarely out of the news, it was not yet the defining issue of our times. While antisemitism was still a significant presence in British life, by the time I was an adolescent it rarely intruded much on the everyday life of Jews like me. We were free to do our own thing, to watch as our communal structures declined into indolence and stagnation. It was home.

Insular and inward-looking gets a bad press. Insular can mean covering up sexual abuse and all manner of horrors. It can mean marginalising and shunning critical voices who would disturb the public image of a community. The Jewish community I grew up in covered up a well-known rabbi with a 'second family', inappropriate relationships between youth leaders and their adolescent charges, endemic financial incompetence. Its culture was conformist and drove away some of our best and brightest.

Today's very public Jewish community, with its very public diversity and its very public dynamism, also conceals things. The outward-facing focus on Israel and antisemitism means that Jewish journalism has relegated everyday Jewish communal news to a lesser role. In my years of working in Jewish communal organisations, I have witnessed untold minor scandals that were never publicly spoken of. Who cares about boring old everyday Jewishness when there are petitions to sign?

In any case, does it necessarily follow that a small-minded, inward-looking, parochial and insular community cannot also be vibrant, alive, self-critical and beautiful? Back in the supposedly somnolent 70s and 80s, my own synagogue was exactly like this. Superficially, we seemed to embody the mediocrity of British Jewry, with our dull building, lousy communal meals and stolid membership. Yet, for much of the 80s, we were also at the cutting edge of Judaism. Our American-born, British-trained rabbi was one of the first women to be ordained in the UK Reform movement. A feminist, she pushed our small 'c' conservative congregation to fully embrace women's participation. She brought into the community LGBT friends, two of whom became the first openly gay female rabbis in the UK. A musician and Yiddishist, she introduced beautiful new tunes into the services. A brilliant mind, her sermons were engaging and challenging. An activist, she was a leading figure in a Jewish campaign for nuclear disarmament. In the few years she was with us, she built up a legacy of members inspired and educated by her, some of whom went on to be rabbis themselves.

This isn't what one would usually think of as parochial and insular, and it's true that we did think about the world beyond our synagogue. But most of what we did, what our rabbi did, was for us. Our synagogue was a world in itself. It had a very limited profile outside the Jewish community, and even in the wider British Jewish community we were fairly obscure. We could have disbanded ourselves and most Jews, let alone non-Jews, would have barely noticed. Even our rabbi's anti-nuclear activism was just a very small drop in a very big pond. There was freedom in that irrelevance.

So yes, a small-minded, inward-looking, parochial and insular community *can* be vibrant, alive, self-critical and beautiful. I want to go further, though, and reclaim another term that most Jews would never think of using ...

Are we a hobby?

I've never known anyone to argue that Jewish life could be classed as a hobby. Surely, we are a civilisation, a way of life, a people, a religion? A hobby is something you do in your spare time, to relax you, to distract you. The (Jewish) philosopher Theodor Adorno, in his famous essay 'Free Time', ridiculed those who asked him whether he had a hobby:

> I take the activities with which I occupy myself beyond the bounds of my official profession, without exception, so seriously that I would be shocked by the idea that they had anything to do with hobbies – that is, activities I'm mindlessly infatuated with only in order to kill time – if my experiences had not toughened me against manifestations of barbarism that have become self-evident and acceptable. Making music, listening to music, reading with concentration constitute an integral element of my existence; the word hobby would make a mockery of them.[2]

While Adorno's essay has sometimes been ridiculed for its curmudgeonly tone, at its heart is a serious critique of the idea of 'free' time and its distractions. Free time and hobbies exist not as a release from the bonds of capitalist work, but to ensure that we have just enough energy to keep the machine running. That sense of leisure as something non-serious, even narcotic, can also be found in Rabbi Abraham Joshua Heschel's much-celebrated work *The Sabbath*, which argues that Shabbat does not exist to make us better workers; we work in order to experience the sacred majesty of the seventh day.[3]

By calling the Jewish way of doing a hobby, I am not lowering the status of Jews; I am raising the status of hobbies. Brian Eno neatly defined art as 'everything you don't have to do', and that definition extends to a vast swathe of other human activities, including hobbies, leisure and free time. In the modern 'Western' world, the freedom to do things we didn't have to do expanded way beyond the idle rich. That freedom was part of a much wider expansion of liberty that included the freedom to be Jewish or not. As such, leisure has in some ways been a threat to Jewish life. The invention of the weekend challenged Shabbat's uniqueness; hobbies and leisure time allowed non-Jewish activities to encroach into Jewish lives. It's no accident that contemporary Haredi Judaism has sought to restrict activities that waste time, given that their entre purpose is to devote their lives to Torah. Leaders of less insular forms of Judaism are acutely aware that they have little choice but to compete for attention in the leisure marketplace.

The idea that Jewish activity could be just another hobby seems to threaten any notion that Judaism and Jewish life have an importance beyond the here and now. That said, as I showed in Chapter Seven, much of what Jews do is doing for the sake of doing. Many of the myriad tasks out of which Jewish life is built are identical to tasks that build other hobby cultures. My father served a term as the treasurer of our synagogue; he also served a term as treasurer of our local theatre and, in retirement, of a volunteer-run library. Books had to balance in exactly the same way. For a while my father collected the first day covers for Israeli stamps. The filing process would have been identical had he been collecting first day covers for Botswanan stamps.

What different hobbies often share is a paradox: The things we don't have to do can be the most important things we do, the things that give us most joy, meaning and fulfilment. At the same time, those things we don't have to do have to be worked at and may require a great deal of mundane drudgery. The effort may be disproportionate to the apparent reward.

Since the early 80s I have been a supporter of Watford Football Club, the team closest to the house where I grew up. For years I had a season ticket with my dad; in my twenties and thirties I no longer went so regularly, but Dad kept on going. Today, I have a season ticket again so I can take my father, now very frail, to matches. My son, whom I raised as a passionate Watford fan, goes as often as he can, as does my nephew. What have we got out of those decades of dedication? Watford had a golden patch for a few years in the 1980s, but subsequently oscillated between the top two divisions, too good to drop into obscurity, too mediocre to achieve greatness. The whole thing has been a complete waste of time; countless hours squashed into uncomfortable seats in the cold, money shelled out to the club every bloody season, horrible traffic jams getting home. The compensations – the fleeting glories, the elemental joy of a well-taken goal, the sense of being part of something – do not outweigh the costs.

The passion and commitment shown by fans of mediocre football teams show that it is possible to build a rich and mean-ingful life around the futile repetition of pointless activity. Just as importantly, it shows you can pass it on to the next genera-tion. While it's glib to talk of fandom as a 'religion', there are certainly lessons Jews can learn from some fan cultures. One of those lessons might be that the reasons Jewish leaders often offer for the decline in Jewish affiliation and activity may not be correct. The reason for the 'crisis' in Jewish continuity is often identified as a failure to pass on meaning, values, ideology and passion. In order to survive, Jewish life needs to be more exciting, extraordinary and innovative. Maybe that's true for some, but the fact that Jewish life can be boring is not necessarily an impediment to Jewish involvement and attachment. Supporting a mediocre football team is, more often than not, achingly dull and mind-numbingly repetitive.

There's something in the small-minded drudgery of hobbies that Jews need to embrace. There's no shortage of small-minded drudgery in Jewish life, but the crucial difference may be a nagging sense that this is not 'enough'; that being and doing Jewish *should* be exciting, and that if we enjoy Jewish drudgery then that is not something to speak of publicly. Judaism and other religions think big and into the next world; by definition they act small in this world since people are small compared to the infinite divine. It is that smallness that makes religions overlap with hobbies, however much they might not want to be categorised as such.

Occasionally, Jews embrace the hobbyistic side of Jewish life and the results can be delightful. A friend of mine once produced a deck of cards, along the lines of the game 'Top Trumps', featuring the founding rebbes of famous Hasidic dynasties. The idea that Hasidic masters could be 'tzimtzumed' into a picture card and assigned a score based on arbitrary criteria acknowledged that Jewish knowledge often accumulates in hobbyistic ways. Other friends of mine, a married couple, have created a self-published magazine called *Private Oy*, which is not just a play on words with the British satirical magazine *Private Eye*, it also copies the format, a mixture of investigative journalism, parody articles and cartoons. *Private Oy* offers deep dives into shady goings on in Jewish charities and dense in-jokes that are only comprehensible to Jewish community geeks. This is a publication with absolutely no public presence beyond its narrow constituency; it turns British Jewish culture into a hobby.

Acknowledgment that Jewish life can be a hobby is rare. I imagine that it would be deeply insulting to those committed to public-facing and idealistic Jewish activism to treat their attempts to change the world as a hobby. The inescapable truth, though, is that these days, most of the time in most places, Jews don't have to be activists. In the US, UK and many other Diaspora Jewish populations, Jews possess the freedom to retreat into private life if they choose. Unlike, for example, my grandmother who joined the communist party when she was young, most Jews are not one step away from grinding poverty and pogroms. However much antisemitism today is a real and growing presence in many Diaspora populations, activism isn't something that we have to do (yet).

Just as it would be absurd to imagine that all humans must be stamp collectors or train spotters, so it is equally bizarre to assume that all Jews will be attracted to the same Jewish hobbies. The Zionist and anti-Zionist hobbies, the progressive and orthodox hobbies, the volunteering hobbies and the apathy hobbies – they are the inevitable consequences of not being forced to do any one Jewish hobby. In societies where there is some personal freedom, the reasons why Jews will sign up to one Jewish ideal or another will always include quirks of taste, personality and leisure-time preferences, as with any other hobby.

Accepting that Jewish idealism and activism can be a hobby is a powerful way of tzimtzuming Jewish politics. It can help us recognise that the reasons Jews disagree with each other may have as much to do with personal taste as deep differences over values. Tzimtzuming our ideals could make us more effective: Instead of the endless futility of proclaiming that our particular take on the world constitutes the essence of Judaism, we could focus on doing our hobby the best way we can and persuading people to join us through making our hobby look attractive. When universities hold society fairs at the start of the year, most would give a wide berth to a society saying that they were the true expression of being a student; smiling, handing out free stuff and seeming like a cool bunch of people to hang out with is a much better strategy.

I want to go further, though. I want to *tzimtzum* the Jews even further; to the point of pure redundancy.

The redundant people

There was a time when I used to say that I didn't want us to be 'Ethno-Religious Group 27b', just another people in a world full of peoples. My reasoning was that, unless we were different and special in some way, Jews may just as well become something else. If Jews were interchangeable with Bulgarian Orthodox Christians, I might as well become a Bulgarian Orthodox Christian.

I now recant this view, but not in a way one might expect: Not only do I want us to become Ethno-Religious Group 27b, I also believe that *this would be the perfect justification for the Jewish people's existence*.

One of the spectres that haunts Jewish existence is *redundancy*. The long history of Christian antisemitism stems in part from 'supersessionism', the idea that God's covenant with the Jewish people has been superseded by a new, universal covenant with humanity via Jesus. Paul famously wrote in Galatians 3:28 that 'There is no longer Jew or Greek, there is no longer slave or free, there is no longer male and female; for all of you are one in Christ Jesus.' Salvation is now for everyone, so the persistence of Jews who refuse it became, as Christianity grew and developed, at best exasperating and at worst diabolic. Jews have no use; they are redundant.

As I pointed out earlier, the longer the Jewish people have survived, the more apparent it has become that other peoples have not. While the Jewish people have earned the right to a modest amount of smugness, there is a sting in the tail of Jewish history when framed this way. By focusing on the rise and fall of civilisations, we also prove that it is possible for entire peoples to vanish into history. Who today remembers the Sogdians? Even Jews who hold to the hope of the Messianic era also know that, while our faithfulness has ensured that the Messiah will come from the lineage of David, it doesn't necessarily mean that there will be much of a Jewish people left to greet him/her/them.

There are many parts of the world where Jews have vanished due to expulsion, murder, assimilation or emigration. While Jews can and should mourn these lost Jewish populations, one of the most difficult lessons they give us is that, for the most part, the peoples who live there now are doing just fine without us. On my 2023 visit to Poland, I encountered a prosperous country with no shortage of cultural and intellectual vibrancy. While there are significant numbers of Poles who are interested in the country's Jewish heritage, for all practical purposes it's possible to live in Poland without the absence of Jews impinging on your life in any way. Even when the loss of Jews also means a loss of something they offered as well, countries recover in time. The *convivienca* of Jews, Christians and Muslims in the Spanish 'golden age' was destroyed even before the expulsion of the Jews and Muslims in 1492. But Spain did get over it in the end and produced Cervantes, Velázquez, Lorca and Julio Iglesias.

Jews have been justifying their existence for almost as long as Jews have existed. Some of that justification is for internal consumption only; given the acute vulnerability of the Jewish people, particularly when we were a purely Diaspora people, Jews needed the comfort of a secure place in the theological firmament. Jewish theology cut no ice with the non-Jewish majority, of course, so our existence needed to be demonstrated rather than justified through metaphysical arguments. We demonstrated our usefulness through the niches we occupied, even though those niches may have been despised ones. As usurers, merchants, doctors and small traders, we leveraged our cultural strengths: our international networks, our literacy, our experience in finding the cracks in society where we might thrive. In the end, though, history shows that however economically and professionally we might be embedded in our host societies, antisemitic hate will sometimes trump self-interest. Medieval English monarchs may have benefited from Jewish money lenders, but once they were expelled in 1290, the monarchy did not collapse.

Today, Jews demonstrate their usefulness in various ways, including finding professional niches as they did before. The 'knowledge economy' builds on historical Jewish traditions of literacy and scholarship. One of the most common tropes in pro-Israel anti-boycott campaigns is to suggest that boycotting Israel would require boycotting iPhones and all manner of other tech that Israel has had a hand in developing.[4] For those who use this argument, the Jewish state is now so comprehensively useful that – finally – Jews have ensured that the world could never dispense with us, however much they might want to.

This Jewish ability to be 'everywhere' is often used to ground antisemitic myths of Jewish power and conspiracy. Really, though, it's a sign of our vulnerability; insecurity that we will be proved redundant leads us to perform our indispensability to whomever will give us the time. As I've argued in this book, we misrepresent ourselves and underplay everyday Jewishness not because we are mendacious, but because this often seems the only way for a small people to survive in a big world.

This strategy may or may not work indefinitely. I am convinced, though, that there is something wrong in principle when Jews clamour to prove our value to the world. Why should we justify our existence? To assert that the Jewish people should 'contribute' something is to come dangerously close to an instrumental view of humanity in which only 'useful' people can justifiably exist. Maybe we can make a better argument for our existence by not making an argument for our existence ...

The pointless people

One of my favourite metal albums is Type O Negative's 1997 release *October Rust*. The inlay photo in the CD features the band looking mean and uncompromising under the words 'FUNCTIONLESS ART IS SIMPLY TOLERATED VANDALISM ... WE ARE THE VANDALS'. I love the defiance with which the band proclaim their lack of useful purpose, eschewing self-justification and embracing performative redundancy. Yet my whole intellectual training taught me that the idea of art that can float free of society, politics and the circumstances of its production is entirely bogus. Even the most abstract paintings or themeless symphonies were born in the world humans make and circulate within it. That's as true of *October Rust* as anything else. Still, I can't help feeling that the assertion of one's own redundancy can still be a radical act, even if it is a fiction. For a Jewish people who are so worldly, it would certainly be shocking to pose as what we have tried so hard not to be. What would it feel like for Jews to assert their pointlessness, their uselessness, their redundancy?

There's something beautiful about existence for its own sake. I have always felt that the ultimate artistic gesture was to create without any desire to show one's work. Similarly, Jews doing for the sake of doing, without any expectation of reward, has a kind of theological integrity to it.

It is but a short step from exulting in this pointlessness to recognising the arbitrary nature of the entire edifice of Jewish life and tradition. The sheer variety of different ways that humans have lived and continue to live makes it very difficult to see the form that the Jewish people now take as somehow pre-ordained.

Against the backdrop of deep time, all we are is an arbitrary assemblage of elements. That's all any group of humans is. Anything we do could always have been otherwise, even if we insist that it couldn't. Our history is so extensive that even minor historical changes could have altered much about what we understand as Jewish today. We aren't so old that someone stepping on a butterfly in ancient Israel could have altered the timeline enough to make pork kosher. We are old enough that there is every possibility that another individual might have prevailed in a labyrinthine argument on Jewish law conducted in ancient Israel, leading to who knows what consequences for liturgy, law and practice.

Isn't there something precious about the fact that the Jewish people have turned out as they are? Recognising this is no different to recognising the wonder of individual uniqueness. That my entire existence derives from one of countless sperm winning the race to one egg makes it feel even more extraordinary that I turned out as I did. I am just one person, the Jews are just one people. I will die and be forgotten eventually, so will every constellation of arbitrary elements be subsumed into the historical memory hole before the sun dies. That is all fine.

This point of view seems to contradict both traditional and progressive Jewish theologies. Yet tacit or open acknowledgment of arbitrariness may be more common than we think. The orthodox woman who taught Judaism at my school made us write down that the laws regarding kosher food have absolutely nothing to do with ancient Jewish health practices. We don't eat lobster because we don't eat lobster, not because shellfish are scavengers and can easily make us sick. The corollary is that Jews today could just as easily be strictly avoiding celery and welcoming in the Sabbath with roast koala. There is a wonderfully obstinate tendency in Judaism to resist reducing Jewish knowledge to 'useful' knowledge. In some orthodox circles, it is seen as particularly praiseworthy to study the laws of Temple sacrifices, even among those who see no imminent prospect of needing them, not despite but because of their lack of immediate utility.[5] Indeed, the concept of *Torah Lishma* (Torah 'for its own sake' and, by implication, 'for the sake of God') is frequently invoked across the Jewish spectrum as an ideal. We study Torah because that's what we do.

Jews are often faced with 'why do we/you do this?' questions, but sometimes there really is no satisfying answer, or the answer is disappointing. In many British progressive communities, most of the second paragraph of the *Aleinu* prayer, which comes at the end of services, is recited in English, while the first paragraph is recited or sung in Hebrew. Why? Insofar as there is a reason, it's likely to be that no one has a good tune for the second paragraph and rabbis are wary of testing their congregants' patience by including too much Hebrew reading. If some bright spark a hundred years ago had come up with a banging tune for the second paragraph maybe we'd be doing the first paragraph in English.

It may well be that recasting Jewish life and Jewish doing as arbitrary and pointless cannot be reconciled with whole swathes of Jewish theology. The contradiction can be resolved in everyday practice, though. Doing Jewish may feel exactly the same to the fervently orthodox and the fervently relativist alike.

There is one issue that seems harder to resolve: Why do Jewish if it's all arbitrary and pointless?

Once you recognise Jewish arbitrariness, the choice becomes not Jewishness versus something more meaningful, but Jewishness versus another arbitrary grab bag of stuff. For those born Jewish, it may simply be easiest to carry on with what you know how to do. Inertia is a great contributor to Jewish continuity. At the same time, Jewish doing can be quite demanding and it's difficult to carry on without some kind of reason to continue. The most effective justification might be more mundane than we think. We already know how to carry on with what we are given in our families. While family members sometimes do become estranged, most remain tied to those we were born with. It would be pretty bizarre to break contact with a sibling only because they are not particularly fun to be around, since siblings don't have to be friends. We work with what we've got. There's something fundamentally righteous about coming to terms with what we are born into, even if we wouldn't choose it. That's how we square the circle, acknowledging both arbitrariness and avoiding the nightmare of a society organised like a buffet where we choose the tastiest-looking thing. Even when people actively choose to be Jewish, the ones who manage this most successfully are often those who accept that, on conversion, you also inherit a large amount of everyday stuff that you might not be thrilled about having to do.

You might object that the young and idealistic need idealistic reasons to be Jewish. But there is an idealism in accepting membership of a people in spite of its flaws, just as there is in accepting one's ties and responsibilities to any group of others. In any case, some traditions continue through the generations perfectly well without any higher ideals. My son embraced Watford Football Club just as I did when my father started taking me, knowing full well that it's neither a glamorous nor successful club. While there are things about the club that I love, ultimately my love of Watford comes down to being a way of distracting myself on the passage between birth and death through arbitrary allegiance with a mediocre assemblage of elements.

What if your hobby is changing the world for the better, though? Should the pointless hobby of Jewish peoplehood shun such people? Well, no, it shouldn't. There are indeed small-minded ways for Jews to make the world a better place.

Small-minded politics

While it's hard not to feel that the world is becoming a more dangerous and scary place, in some of the small worlds I have been involved in, something remarkable has happened.

On my recent visits to watch Watford be irredeemably mediocre on the pitch, off the pitch I have seen things I never thought I'd see. The club now has a sensory room designed for neurodiverse people to watch the match in a more manageable location. I've seen a rainbow flag, proudly waved by LGBT supporters. I've seen hotlines set up to report racist comments in the crowd. Without much fanfare, the club has sought to ensure that Watford is for everyone. This has happened at a time during which the team itself has been in a state of chaos, a joke to many as the owners change managers every few months in search of elusive success.

In my heavy-metal life, I've also seen the unimaginable. As recently as the early 2000s, when I began publishing the results of my PhD research, I was reconciled to metal being a space that might tolerate women, LGBT people and non-white groups, but would never really embrace the possibility of a more diverse scene. Since then, I have witnessed metal feminism becoming a thing, LGBT metal podcasts, anti-fascist black metal activism and mental-health charities setting up stalls at metal festivals. While there is still plenty of pushback, metal is on the way to becoming a culture for everyone who loves distorted power chords.

Here's what I haven't seen, though: I haven't seen anyone claim that, when Watford Football Club was set up in 1881, its essence was a desire for social justice and inclusion. Sure, Watford got into the inclusion game earlier than most. In the 1970s and 80s under Graham Taylor's managership and Elton John's chairmanship, it positioned itself as a club for all. Witnessing opposing fans abuse our openly gay chairman may have taught us to revile homophobia. Watford has become what it is through evolution and the choices that its staff and fans made; the club was not destined to be this way.

Metal's destiny was also not preordained. The music and its culture are based on a canon produced from the late 60s onwards by performers who were marinated in sexism and systematically erased the blues – and blackness – from the emerging genre. The politically progressive elements in today's metal culture do not deny the problematic inheritance on which they seek to build. Sure, some may want to rebuild metal on different principles, but that doesn't imply historical amnesia. Sure, some may find in metal's celebration of freedom an inspiration for a freedom beyond that imagined by its foundational artists, but there is no getting away from the ambivalence of the debt we owe them.

It's possible to achieve social change in small worlds without implying that this was always the essential purpose of those worlds. There is a sense of proportion in these worlds I love dearly and I am thrilled with how far they've come. In a world with innumerable other worlds contained within it, it is in those more modest spaces that real social change can be incubated. That modesty is important: The eyes of the entire world are not on Watford FC nor on metal shows in dive bars. Those who push for and achieve hard-won change are also fans who love the culture and don't believe that absolutely everyone has to share it. If there is hope in the world, it is here, in thousands of spaces that exist for themselves yet contribute to something bigger without really intending to.

I've seen change in the Jewish world in my lifetime. As a kid, women rabbis were a novelty even in the progressive Jewish world; now some orthodox denominations are starting to ordain them. The needs of Jews with disabilities, Jews of colour, trans Jews and those struggling with mental-health issues are becoming standard parts of the communal conversation. I have also seen the reverse, as fundamentalist Jewish groups grew in power in Israel; indeed, for pretty much every belief I have, I can find a Jew who would find it disgusting. Still, my immediate Jewish surroundings are much more inclusive than when I first encountered them.

The problem is the overselling, the pretensions of Jewish activists to promulgate the essence of Jewishness. That overblown rhetoric, together with the tendency of Jews to take a very public place at the vanguard of movement after movement, is what threatens to overwhelm us. The lessons of Watford FC and metal are that it is possible to have ideals, to put them into action, without eating up everything else in the process.

We would benefit from taking the discourse down a notch. When Watford installed the sensory room they didn't proclaim it to be an act of *tikkun olam*. So much of social justice activism, when shorn of idealistic verbiage, simply comes down to the mundane work of making communities open to diverse kinds of people. Installing disabled ramps or making black people feel welcome is not, when it comes down to it, that dramatic, even though it can involve an initial period of adjustment. Ultimately, it's just self-interest, since inclusion makes us bigger. The same goes for solidarity with oppressed groups. Given our historical experience it's hardly surprising that some Jews today will identify with Palestinian suffering and that some Jews in the 60s took part in the civil-rights movement. It's also unsurprising that other Jews will have taken very different lessons from their historical experience and make common cause with other groups. Why does the human tendency to find allies and enemies need to be dressed up as more?

If we saw ourselves as just another arbitrary assemblage of elements we could see ourselves as compelled to change the world because the world needs to be changed, not because it's our destiny. We are just one interchangeable set of humans who have to play their part in a much bigger process. If I was Bulgarian orthodox I'd be supporting female priests and gay marriage in Bulgarian orthodox churches. It just happens that by chance I am Jewish, so I support female rabbis and gay marriage in synagogues.

The small-minded Jewish politics I am advocating is not just about prioritising the Jewish sector of a wider battle-ground; it's also about paying attention to our own parochial politics. Jews need to engage politically for some very mundane, and largely uncontroversial, reasons. For example, every few years in the UK, a proposal is floated to shorten the length of the school summer holidays and redistribute the days more evenly across the year. If this adjustment were to happen, it would cause real issues with Jewish summer camps and Israel tours for young people as, in the summer break, parents would have to choose between a family holiday and sending their kids away. Jewish representative organisations lobby government on such issues. This kind of Jewish politicking seems like special pleading out of parochial self-interest – and this is exactly what it is and that's absolutely fine. My concern, though, is that a Jewish community so constantly in the public eye regarding 'big' issues will lose interest in and neglect the everyday stuff of Jewish politics.

'Parochial' can be a dirty word, a synonym for myopic triviality. It really shouldn't be. The fact is that my own Jewish life, and that of many others, is as directly impacted by the internecine politics within Jewish organisations that shape my life as it is by big issues such as antisemitism and Israel–Palestine. Votes by obscure trustees of Jewish organisations are as significant to me as votes in parliament. Actually, in some ways, small-minded politics may be more consequential than any other politics. You may hate a prime minister or a president, but most likely you will never meet them. If you hate your synagogue rabbi your life is inextricably linked with theirs, with all the potential for misery that this implies.

Small-minded politics will be with us as long as small worlds exist. That is neither a good nor bad thing; it's just a thing. But when small-minded politics is relegated to second place or to no place at all, it sends the message that everyday life is unimportant compared to the *real* issues. Since at least 7 October 2023, this message that mundane Jewish life is of secondary interest at best seems to be prevailing. In the Jewish media, in the UK, the US and in many other countries, antisemitism, Israel and related issues dominate coverage. Board-level coups, furious schisms and the other minutiae of small-minded politics are relegated to the middle of the paper (figuratively or literally). Until we *tzimtzum* ourselves, we risk becoming completely assimilated into the grandeur of meta-politics.

Will making ourselves smaller stop antisemitism?
No.

Oh, you can do better than that ...
Well, all right then ... maybe in time a *tzimtzum*ed Jewish people might become too unimportant to hate. But by 'time' here, I mean decades, centuries, millennia. We aren't newcomers to the being-hated business. There's a bountiful 'reservoir' of antisemitic ideas and tropes that has been filling up over millennia, largely unacknowledged, that is just waiting to be used when non-Jews have even a minor beef with Jews.[6] Other peoples have been the subject of hatred and racism for a transitory period before vanishing from the cultural imagination. There was a time when Maltese Londoners were associated with pimping and sexual predation; no longer. There was a time when Protestants and Catholics routinely slaughtered each other; now even Northern Ireland is calming down. Frankly, I don't see us losing our hateability or (to some) our lovability; we are too important to forget, for the foreseeable future, anyway.

The reasons why I advocate reducing ourselves and our politics has nothing to do with fighting antisemitism. But it does have a lot to do with *surviving* antisemitism.

In an article published in April 2024, Howard Jacobson shared his fears that the war in Gaza was leading to the abandonment of both Israel and the Jewish people:

> I fear they – papers and commentators and politicians – are losing interest and sympathy at the same rate. They've heard it all before. We Jews need to find other ways to make our

harrowing history compelling. We've tried losing. We've tried winning. I'm not sure what's left.[7]

Jacobson's piece was symptomatic of how many Jews today can't even imagine a smaller approach to Jewish politics. The investment in public Jewishness is now so deep that smallness connotes craven surrender. The desire for friendship and sympathy is so profound that we cannot even conceive how our 'harrowing history' might be received as one among other harrowing histories. Nor does the idea that we might be able to make alliances with those who feel nothing for our history seem to cross Jewish minds.

Again and again I've seen the words of Elie Wiesel shared by Jews on social media:

The opposite of love is not hate, it's indifference.
The opposite of art is not ugliness, it's indifference.
The opposite of faith is not heresy, it's indifference.
And the opposite of life is not death, it's indifference.[8]

Empirically, psychologically, philosophically and sociologically, I am not sure that this is true. I definitely believe that, as the basis for a political strategy, fighting indifference raises the bar absurdly high. Given that politicians are some of the most cynical people in the world – they have to be – are we really saying that Jewish survival is dependent on them *caring*? In any case, while care may be endless in theory, attention is limited in practice. Given the state of the world, do we have to care about everybody and everything? I don't think there are enough hours in the day.

We need to try fighting antisemitism in a more matter of fact, more instrumental way, giving the world pragmatic reasons to stop plundering the antisemitic reservoir. Not only is the idealistic approach setting the bar too high, a world in which 'everyone' cared about our 'harrowing history' would be a world in which being and doing Jewish would be entirely subsumed into a greater narrative. As this book has shown, we are already well on the way to that baleful situation.

To treat everyday Jewishness as trivial is to ignore the only 'prize' that can be won by vanquishing antisemitism. In a world without antisemitism, Jews will find that the pot of gold at the end of the rainbow is the ability to be and do Jewish without being hated for it. Such a world would also be one where Jews would become much less interesting to non-Jews. We would become a small people. It would be an anticlimax. That's fine with me.

It's rare for Jews to talk about the anticlimactic 'rewards' of not being hated. One wonderful exception can be found in the British journalist Daniel Finkelstein's book *Hitler, Stalin, Mum and Dad*.[9] Finkelstein's parents barely survived the horrors of the mid-twentieth century. His father Ludwig was deported as a child with his mother by the Soviets when they took over Lvov/ Lvyv/Lemburg following the Nazi–Soviet pact. Forced to live with barely any food in a makeshift house made of cow dung on the freezing plains of Kazakhstan, they somehow survived and were eventually reunited with Ludwig's father, who had been deported to Siberia. The family made their way first to Iran, then to Palestine and England. Finkelstein's mother's family had fled from Germany to Amsterdam in the 1930s (her father was a Jewish political activist and had fled to London by the time war broke out) and they were was deported via Westerbork to Bergen-Belsen. They just about survived as 'prominent' prisoners who was released to Switzerland after much lobbying by her father's friends.

Extraordinary stuff, to be sure. But this is how Finkelstein sums up his family's history at the start of the book:

> This is a story of love and murder. A story of how the great forces of history crashed down in a terrible wave on two happy families; of how it tossed them and turned them, and finally returned what was left to dry land. It's a story of brilliant ingenuity, great bravery and almost unbelievable coincidences. It's a story of secret archives and freezing wastelands; of forgery and theft; concentration camps and the Gulag. Of evil and the consequences of evil. And of freedom, and freedom's reward. It's the story of how my family took a journey which ended happily in Hendon, eating crusty bread rolls with butter in the Tesco café near the M1, but on the way took a detour through hell.[10]

'Freedom's reward' was dull suburban life. Finkelstein could have emphasised that, even in the UK, his parents remained stubbornly extraordinary (his father Ludwig became a well-respected engineer and academic and completed a PhD in Jewish studies on retirement; his wife Mirjam was also an accomplished scientist at a time when women were uncommon in science); he chose to emphasise the crusty bread rolls with butter in Tesco. Ludwig and Mirjam Finkelstein had successfully *tzimtzum*ed.

Perhaps it takes a truly horrific experience to yearn for mundane insignificance. One of the difficulties in fighting antisemitism is that the very fact that we can fight so publicly is taken as proof that the phenomenon isn't that serious. For the most part, antisemitism as it is usually experienced today impacts more on Jewish being than on Jewish doing. I can understand why some Jews might think that acknowledging that Jewish everyday life is fairly resilient would weaken the fight against antisemitism. Nonetheless, this wariness does not really help us in the long-term. The tendency to clamour for extraordinary significance will, in the end, devour us.

So, to answer Howard Jacobson's rhetorical question, there is something Jews haven't tried. It's time to see what it would be like for Jews to proudly embrace a new identity, as people who follow an arbitrary hobby for the sake of it, without any greater purpose than that. It's time for non-Jews who see themselves as our friends to let us be insignificant.

Why not give it a go? You might even like it.

Conclusion

A desperate rearguard attempt to demonstrate my
intellectual credentials

As I was finishing writing this book, I came across a 1973 quotation from Gershom Scholem that, at first glance, unnerved me in how far – and how much better – it seemed to sum up my own view:

> We are not obliged to justify our existence by working for the world. Nobody, no other nation, has ever been put under such an obligation, and some of us see it as scandalous that unlike everyone else, we have to justify being Jews by serving some further purpose. No one asks a Frenchman why he is there. Everyone asks a Jew why he is there; no one would be content with the statement, I am just a Jew. Yet the Jew has every right to be just a Jew and to contribute to what he is by being just what he is.[1]

Just when I thought my entire book was redundant, I continued reading:

> We are always asked to be something exceptional, something supreme, something ultimate. Maybe that very expectation

> will come to fruition one day, and perhaps then even the
> enigma of being the chosen people, which is not so easily
> discarded, will be resolved.[2]

Scholem, while perhaps exasperated by the demand that Jews justify themselves, also holds out the possibility that at some point we might be able to do so. As one of Judaism's greatest scholars and an authority of Judaism's mystical tradition, it was perhaps too difficult to fully accept that it was all an arbitrary and pointless game.

I found the quote in the epigraph to Adam Sutcliffe's 2020 book *What are Jews for?*, which I'd been meaning to read since it was published. The book shows how debates over the purpose of Jews and Judaism are of great antiquity and resonate to this day. He shows how even 'secular' Jews today often draw on unacknowledged legacies of ideas of 'chosenness'. While Jewish purpose may be understood as of universal relevance or of particularist relevance just for Jews, what different visions of Jewish purpose share is a desire for *hope*:

> If Jewish purpose can be distilled to one word, then the
> choice is clear. Jews are for hope. Hope for what, though?
> This question takes us back to our point of departure: God's
> twice-forged covenant with Abraham and Moses. God
> chose the Jews, but seemed to leave to them, and equally
> to everyone else, the task of figuring out why. The history
> of the Jewish purpose question sets out, in rich complexity,
> the various interconnected human attempts to answer that
> question. It cannot, though, provide any definitive answer.[3]

Reflecting on Sutcliffe's book and its epigraph, I was very conscious that, while my interests are similar to him, my approach is different, almost brutally so. Instead of Sutcliffe's elegant intellectual history, I offer everyday Jewish doing as a kind of 'solution' to the question of what Jews are for, even though the ones doing the doing may not realise it. I counterpose what we do to what we think to the extent that my argument seems anti-intellectual. On top of that, I seem to be indifferent to the need for hope. Purposeless and hopeless – what on earth have I written? How did it come to this?

A confession

Every fibre of my being tells me that the Jewish people are extraordinary and interesting. Our traditions are rich and beautiful. We have uniquely important things to say and Jewish values and ideals are worth fighting for. The world would look different without us.

And here I am arguing that we should ignore all of this.

I arrived at the unexpected point because these are the most difficult times I have experienced in my life. Jewishly, I am in despair at what is happening in Israel–Palestine, but there's much more to it than that. Climate change, the rise of authoritarianism, price rises, austerity and so much more. It's very hard to be optimistic right now.

I don't need – *we* don't need – the Jewish people to be in the vanguard of the struggle to get through what is coming. I certainly don't want the struggle to be reducible to a Jewish struggle (or an anti-Jewish one). We are all going to need some kind of haven in the years to come. By that I don't mean a place where we ignore the world outside or deny the seriousness of our times. I mean a place where the struggle becomes manageable.

Tzimtzum, the sacred reduction that I discussed in the previous chapter, is based on a conceit that God can be anything other than infinite. So it is that this book experiments with the conceit of treating Jews as less interesting than they actually are. I wanted to see what it would be like to base Jewish life on nothing more than everyday Jewish doing. I wanted to see what it would be like to treat my heritage as if it were nothing more than an arbitrary set of symbols, practices and actions.

Frankly, I'm starting to like it. This is where the hope lies: That this intense pressure on us to be significant will ease, pretence be damned.

Making Jews smaller has helped me to focus on what I value most about being and doing Jewish. It turns out that Jewish tradition and Jewish people, once stripped of the robes of importance, are a wonderful thing! I adore the obscure knottiness of ancient Jewish texts, the baroque circumlocutions of *halacha*, the specificities of Anglo-Jewish dialect and the joy of fried gefilte fish balls. Why do I need anything more? Why does any of it need to be *about* anything but itself? Ironically, making Jews smaller could do much more to preserve the wonderful treasures of Jewish tradition than any number of bombastic statements of our tragic significance.

For so long we have misrepresented ourselves and been misrepresented by others as more than we are. Now is the time to misrepresent ourselves as less than we are. We are going to need some help. I certainly can't lead the struggle. I am not a writer of sufficient stature to shift the way millions of Jews see themselves, let alone the non-Jewish multitudes. In any case, it isn't entirely up to Jews to decide how and whether to accept Jewish mundanity. It isn't just Jews who fall for the seductiveness of the extraordinary, the important and the significant. There is a much deeper problem at work here. If Jews are, as the cliche goes, the 'canary in the coalmine' for anything, it may be this ...

Pay attention!

Since the early 70s, psychologists and economists have been talking about the 'attention economy'. Like any other resource, humans have a finite amount of attention they can 'spend'. In complex capitalist societies, any enterprise – whether it be business, a campaign, a religion or a hobby – depends on attracting and keeping the attention of its 'customers'. While I am wary of such economistic analogies, it's hard to deny that the competition for attention is a profoundly important dynamic in society. Further, in the age of social media the sheer amount of competition has grown to an extraordinary degree, and holding attention has become ever more difficult.[4]

The Jewish people are haunted by the consequences of *inattention*. It's an over-simplification to suggest that the Holocaust and other horrors that Jews experienced occurred because the world was 'distracted' and didn't pay enough attention to us. It's also understandable why many Jews might see it that way. Similarly, it's understandable that Palestinians and their advocates might also see their struggle as a struggle for attention.

Everyday life always struggles to receive attention unless it is particularly quirky or harmful. The attention economy is also an importance economy, and it's hard to make gefilte fish sound important. Inevitably, the competition for importance leads to a situation where what we are fighting for – the 'prize' I mentioned in the previous chapter – becomes obscured. Whole sides of ourselves, the everyday sides, risk lapsing into neglect. That is everyone's problem. We are going to have to fight for everyday life if we don't want to become shells of human beings endlessly competing for likes.

In a world of clamour, cacophony and narcissism, we are all going to need to *tzimtzum*, to reduce ourselves to something that is actually worth preserving. Here we face another problem – what happens when the world changes so radically that the everyday life we used to rely on is swept away?

Back to normal

There were Jews ensnared by the Nazis during the Holocaust who, amid their suffering, dreamed of a better world to be built from the ruins of the old. I always thought that, if I was ever in a similar situation, I would be one of those Jews. I realise now that I am with the Jews who just wanted things to go back to normal, however impossible that was.

I didn't think I was a particularly nostalgic person, but in recent years I have had an intense desire to *return*. As the years pass, the return date changes. During the political turmoil of 2019, I yearned for 2015, the time before Brexit and Trump. During the pandemic I would have settled for 2019. Today, the certainties of lockdown seem appealing. Frankly, it's been so long since the smugly placid 1990s that I am losing touch with what normality actually felt like, if it ever existed in the first place.

As the world careers out of control, nostalgia will not save us. We can't go back and, given that the past sowed the seeds of the now, we shouldn't want to go back. Yet there's still a shred of normality that we need to save from the wreckage: the mundane experience of everyday life. Even post-normality we might, if we try, still be able to experience boredom, mediocrity and ragged tatters of the banal. We will have to fight for it. In an extraordinary age we will have to rebuild our ordinariness from the ground up.

Jews offer both precedents to avoid and models to follow. We are a cautionary tale of a people that is currently being dragged into a state of extraordinariness. We are also a people that has a broad and deep tradition of everyday doing. Our love of mundane organising and doing for the sake of doing can be a model for a resilient normality. However much we might be losing sight of this right now, there are many historical precedents of Jews preserving the ordinary in the face of turbulent reality.

Perhaps this is one struggle in which Jews and everyone else can share in: We need you to fight for your everydayness just as we have to fight for ours. No one is mundane unless everyone can be mundane.

Support your local Jews

This book is not part of a PR campaign. I am a firm believer in washing our dirty laundry in public. While there might be some aspects of Jewish life discussed in this book that appeal to non-Jews, it's not my intention to beguile.

Still, if you really want to help the Jews, there might be some things you can do. Here's what you might want to try if you live in the UK.

Find a local synagogue online.

Email them to ask if you can attend a service.

After the email bounces back to say no such address exists, resend it.

After you give up sending emails, ring the synagogue office.

Leave a message on the answer machine.

After a few days, ring again and leave another message.

When you finally get through, try and allay the synagogue secretary's suspicions by mentioning the instructions in this book. He or she will never have heard of me, even though I am due to give a talk at the synagogue that evening.

Give up getting permission and resolve just to turn up on Shabbat morning.

Turn up at 9.30am on Shabbat, walk past person on security rota who looks straight through you.

If it's an orthodox synagogue, services will have already started, there will only be a few people there and the service leader will be mumbling while the congregation chats. No one will greet you.

If it's a progressive synagogue, services will not have started yet. There might be a class for resentful adolescents somewhere else in the building. No one will greet you.

Watch people wander in in desultory fashion. You will still be ignored.

At some point, rabbi walks past and nods at you. Enjoy this experience.

Service happens. Do as Jews do and spend most of the time looking at who else has come to service.

When the service ends, rush into the hall next to the prayer space and be first at the table for kiddush.

Wait for blessing over bread and wine. This will take a long time, and in the meantime several old ladies will have somehow pushed past you.

Eat bamba, eat cookies. Desperately try and counteract dryness by swigging syrup-sweet kiddush wine.

Find sign-up sheet for supper quiz. Notice that it took place last week.

Resolve to try Bulgarian orthodoxy next week.

The end.

So, how are we going to survive this?
Like that.

Endnotes

A note on language
1. Kahn-Harris, K. (2018) 'Factsheet: Judaism in Britain', *Religion Media Centre*, 18 April. Available at: https://religionmediacentre.org.uk/factsheets/judaism-in-britain/ (Accessed: 24 July 2024).

Introduction
1. Nirenberg, D. (2013) *Anti-Judaism: The Western Tradition*. W. W. Norton.
2. Ward, J. (2014) *Adventures in Stationery: A Journey Through Your Pencil Case*. Profile Books.
3. Kahn-Harris, K. (2021) *The Babel Message: A Love Letter to Language*. Icon Books.
4. Kahn-Harris, K. (2006) *Extreme Metal: Music and Culture on the Edge*. Oxford: Berg.

Chapter One: Baseball in the bloodlands
1. Heimann, F. and Sulzenbacher, H. (eds) (2022) *'Ausgestopfte Juden?' Geschichte, Gegenwart und Zukunft Jüdischer Museen*. ['Stuffed Jews?' History, present and future of Jewish museums] Göttingen: Wallstein Verlag.
2. Kahn-Harris, K. (2023) 'The Holocaust as void', *A Curious Miscellany*, 22 May. Available at:

https://keithkahnharris.substack.com/p/the-holocaust-as-void (Accessed: 24 July 2024).

3. The archive is free to access and can be found at: https://www.jpr.org.uk/archive

4. Kahn-Harris, K. and Boyd, J. (2023) *The field of research on contemporary antisemitism and Jewish life: Working towards a European research hub*. Brussels: European Commission.

5. Fackenheim, E.L. (1987) *The Jewish Thought of Emil Fackenheim: A Reader*. Wayne State University Press: 157–83.

6. Horn, D. (2021) *People Love Dead Jews: Reports from a Haunted Present*. W. W. Norton & Company.

Chapter Two: The secrets of the Jews

1. Jacobson, H. (2023) *Is it time for Jews to do less yearning and more living?* 2 March 2023. Available at: https://www.thejc.com/lets-talk/is-it-time-for-jews-to-do-less-yearning-and-more-living-vt6xu3fu (Accessed: 24 July 2024).

2. Lebrecht, N. (2019) *Genius & Anxiety: How Jews Changed the World, 1847–1947*. Simon and Schuster: 3.

3. Baum, D. (2017) *Feeling Jewish: (A Book for Just About Anyone)*. Yale University Press: 249.

4. 'Stephen Fry Addresses the Nation' (25 December 2023). Available at: https://www.youtube.com/watch?v=G7uUGJhiehM (Accessed: 24 July 2024).

5. 'Alexei Sayle's Alternative Alternative Christmas Message' (25 December 2023). Available at: https://www.youtube.com/watch?v=jnbDn3ghqbk (Accessed: 24 July 2024).

6. The speech was used as an official trailer for the series: 'The Marvelous Mrs. Maisel – Official Trailer' (10

October 2017). Available at: https://www.youtube.com/watch?v=fOmwkTrW4OQ (Accessed: 25 July 2024).

7. Season 4, episode 5.

8. *Growing Up Jewish* screened on 24 April 2024.

9. Mangan, L. (2024) '*Growing Up Jewish* review – wildly inappropriately lightweight for our times', *Guardian*, 24 April. Available at: https://www.theguardian.com/tv-and-radio/2024/apr/24/growing-up-jewish-review-wildly-inappropriately-lightweight-for-our-times (Accessed: 25 July 2024).

10. Chernick, D. (no date) 'Growing Up Jewish – The BBC One b'mitzvah documentary', *Growing Up Jewish – The BBC One b'mitzvah documentary | JIGGLE.IN*. Available at: https://www.jiggle.in/blog/post/21847/growing-up-jewish--the-bbc-one-bmitzvah-documentary/ (Accessed: 25 July 2024).

Chapter Three: The Jewification game

1. https://www.youtube.com/watch?v=qtgJQ5YD2uE (Accessed: 11 August 2024).

2. Yapalater, L. (2023) *43 Jewish Celebrities You Might Not Have Known Were Jewish*, BuzzFeed. Available at: https://www.buzzfeed.com/lyapalater/celebrities-that-you-didnt-realize-were-jewish (Accessed: 25 July 2024).

3. 'Category: Jewish heavy metal musicians' (2024), Wikipedia. Available at: https://en.wikipedia.org/w/index.php?title=Category:Jewish_heavy_metal_musicians&oldid=1227643378 (Accessed: 25 July 2024).

4. Recordings of Matzo and Metal can sometimes be found on YouTube, such as: https://youtu.be/KwzbiKRTaIk?si=U1n1RP1QFAKZerEE (Accessed: 25 July 2024).

5. Kahn-Harris, K. (2010) 'How Diverse Should Metal Be? The Case of Jewish Metal, Overt and Covert Jewishness', in N.W.R. Scott and I. Von Helden (eds) *The Metal Void: First Gatherings*. Oxford: Inter-Disciplinary Press, pp. 110–19.
6. Abrams, N. (2018) *Stanley Kubrick: New York Jewish Intellectual*. Rutgers University Press.
7. Abrams, N. (ed.) (2008) *Jews and Sex*. Nottingham: Five Leaves Publications.
8. Abrams, N. and Friel, D. (2014) 'Outlaw Jews', *Jewish Quarterly*, 61(3–4), pp. 92–93.
9. 'Jonathan Miller: "I'm not prepared to be Jewish in the face of other Jews".' Available at: https://www.youtube.com/watch?v=-2GwIVFE-gs&t=23s (Accessed: 25 July 2024).
10. *The Jewish Chronicle* (2019) 'Sir Jonathan Miller, director, broadcaster and writer, dies at 85', 7 November. Available at: https://www.thejc.com/news/sir-jonathan-miller-director-broadcaster-and-writer-dies-at-85-n4xelz5t (Accessed: 25 July 2024).
11. This is the 'Community Translation' from the Jewish text website *Sefaria*: https://www.sefaria.org/Unetaneh_Tokef.4?lang=bi&with=all&lang2=en (Accessed: 25 July 2024).
12. Barton, J. (2024) 'An Inch Deep and a Mile Wide, or Vice Versa', *Jewish Review of Books*, 15 July. Available at: https://jewishreviewofbooks.com/the-arts/16805/an-inch-deep-and-a-mile-wide-or-vice-versa/ (Accessed: 24 July 2024).
13. 'Jewish and Goyish' (no date) *My Jewish Learning*. Available at: https://www.myjewishlearning.com/culture/2/Humor/History/In_America/WizardsofWit/A_Humor_Perspective/jewishandgoyish.shtml (Accessed: 25 July 2024).

14. Glancy, J. (2023) 'Why everything in the world can be divided into "Jewish or Goyish"', *Jewish Chronicle*, 15 June. Available at: https://www.thejc.com/news/why-everything-in-the-world-can-be-divided-into-jewish-or-goyish-ab6dl4tx (Accessed: 25 July 2024).

15. Abrams, N. (2020) 'The Secret Jewishness of "Broken Wear"', *Nathan Abrams*, 15 April. Available at: https://nathanabrams.wordpress.com/2020/04/15/the-secret-jewishness-of-broken-wear/ (Accessed: 25 July 2024).

Chapter Four: Frailty in numbers

1. Arno, R. (2022) 'In wild overestimate, Americans think 30% of the country is Jewish', *The Forward*, 16 March. Available at: https://forward.com/news/484069/in-wild-overestimate-americans-think-30-of-the-country-is-jewish/ (Accessed: 25 July 2024).

2. DellaPergola, S. (2023) 'World Jewish Population, 2022', in A. Dashefsky and I.M. Sheskin (eds) *American Jewish Year Book 2022: The Annual Record of the North American Jewish Communities Since 1899*. Cham: Springer International Publishing, pp. 291–402. Available at: https://doi.org/10.1007/978-3-031-33406-1_7.

3. JPS 2006 translation.

4. Revised JPS translation 2023.

5. Berakhot 58a, Koren-Steinsaltz translation.

6. Gerim 1:1, 1965 Soncino translation.

7. Axelrod, T. (2022) 'Are too many Germans converting to Judaism? The debate is roiling Germany's Jewish community', *Jewish Telegraphic Agency*, 6 September. Available at: https://www.jta.org/2022/09/06/global/are-too-many-germans-converting-to-judaism-the-debate-is-

roiling-germanys-jewish-community (Accessed: 25 July 2024).

8. Heilman, S.C. (2000) *Defenders of the Faith: Inside Ultra-Orthodox Jewry*. Berkeley: University of California Press: 298.

9. Staetsky, L.D. (2022) *Haredi Jews around the world: Population trends and estimates*. London: European Jewish Demography Unit, Institute for Jewish Policy Research. Available at: https://archive.jpr.org.uk/object-2673 (Accessed: 5 June 2024).

10. Hart, M.B. (2000) *Social Science and the Politics of Modern Jewish Identity*. Stanford, CA.: Stanford University Press.

11. Batorski, P. (20 January 1942) 'The Wannsee Conference seals the fate of European Jews', Żydowski Instytut Historyczny. Available at: https://www.jhi.pl/en/articles/january-20-1942-wannsee-conference,4830 (Accessed: 25 July 2024).

12. Trunk, I. (1996) *Judenrat: The Jewish Councils in Eastern Europe Under Nazi Occupation*. University of Nebraska Press, p. 174.

13. Grzybowski, A. and Pawlikowska-Łagód, K. (2023) 'Izrael Milejkowski and Hunger Disease Study in the Warsaw Ghetto', *Clinics in Dermatology*, 41(1), pp. 159–65. Available at: https://doi.org/10.1016/j.clindermatol.2022.11.004.

14. Available at: https://global100.adl.org/map

Chapter Five: Punching below our weight

1. If you are brave enough, you can find the original video at: https://www.youtube.com/watch?v=qSJCSR4MuhU (Accessed: 25 July 2024).

2. Some of this section has been adapted from my article from 2022, 'Jewish velvet – a touching memoire', *JewThink*, 12 October. Available at: https://www. jewthink.org/2022/10/12/jewish-velvet-a-touching-memoire/ (Accessed: 25 July 2024).

3. Kahn-Harris, K. (2020) 'A Gloriously Miserable British Sukkot', *JewThink*, 9 October. Available at: https://www. jewthink.org/2020/10/09/a-gloriously-miserable-british-sukkot/ (Accessed: 25 July 2024).

Chapter Six: Living and dying to organise

1. Fax, J.G. (2023) *Urgent Campaign Records Eyewitness Accounts of Antisemitic Terror Attacks in Israel, USC Shoah Foundation.* Available at: https://sfi.usc. edu/news/2023/12/35786-urgent-campaign-records-eyewitness-accounts-antisemitic-terror-attacks-israel (Accessed: 25 July 2024).

2. *National Library of Israel Launches Initiative to Preserve October 7 Massacre and War Documentation* (2023). Available at: https://www.nli.org.il/en/at-your-service/ announcements/7-october-documentation-initiative (Accessed: 25 July 2024).

3. Jordan, E. (2024) 'JW3 creates a lovelock bridge for the hostages', *Jewish Chronicle*, 9 February. Available at: https://www.thejc.com/community/jw3-creates-a-lovelock-bridge-for-the-hostages-yz9tuxlb (Accessed: 25 July 2024).

4. 'New initiative invites individuals, groups abroad to "adopt" towns victimized on Oct. 7' (2023) *The Rimes of Israel*, 15 November. Available at: https://www.timesofisrael.com/liveblog_entry/ new-initiative-invites-individuals-groups-abroad-to-adopt-towns-victimized-on-oct-7/ (Accessed: 25 July 2024).

5. https://www.collectifdu7octobre.org/ (Accessed: 25 July 2024).

6. https://www.z3project.org/, https://globaljewry.org/ (Both accessed: 25 July 2024).

7. https://writingonthewall.io/ (Accessed: 25 July 2024).

8. https://www.the10-7project.com/ (Accessed: 25 July 2024).

9. https://www.standing-together.org/en (Accessed: 25 July 2024).

10. https://www.ourjewishvalues.org.uk/ (Accessed: 25 July 2024).

11. Trunk, I. (1996) *Judenrat: The Jewish Councils in Eastern Europe Under Nazi Occupation*. University of Nebraska Press.

12. Ibid., p. 75.

13. Hájková, A. (2020) *The Last Ghetto: An Everyday History of Theresienstadt*. Oxford University Press, p. 58.

14. Foucault, M. (1977) *Discipline and Punish*. Translated by A. Sheridan. London: Penguin Books; Graeber, D. (2015) *The Utopia of Rules: On Technology, Stupidity and the Secret Joys of Bureaucracy*. Brooklyn: Melville House; Weber, M. (1964) *The Theory of Social and Economic Organisation*. Edited by T. Parsons. New York: Free Press.

15. Bauman, Z. (2013) *Modernity and the Holocaust*. John Wiley & Sons.

16. Kassow, S.D. (2007) *Who Will Write Our History?: Emanuel Ringelblum, the Warsaw Ghetto, and the Oyneg Shabes Archive*. Annotated edition. Bloomington (Ind.): Indiana University Press, p. 338.

17. Ibid., p. 242.

18. Casale Mashiah, D. (2019) 'Income Concentration Trends and Competition in the Charitable Sector: An Analysis of Jewish Charities in England and Wales', *Contemporary*

Jewry [Preprint]. Available at: https://archive.jpr.org.uk/object-uk514 (Accessed: 16 March 2024).

19. Kahn-Harris, K. (2021) 'Into the flatlands with Professor David Miller', *JewThink*, 22 February. Available at: https://www.jewthink.org/2021/02/22/into-the-flatlands-with-professor-david-miller/ (Accessed: 25 July 2024).

Chapter Seven: What's the point of it all?

1. https://www.templebeth-el.net/ (Accessed: 25 July 2024).

2. Douglas, M. (2012) *In the Active Voice*. London: Routledge, p. 105.

3. Cohen, S.M. and Eisen, A.M. (2000) *The Jew Within: Self, Family and Community in America*. Bloomington: University of Indiana Press.

4. JPS 2006 translation.

5. This comes from an email that circulated among Jewish education types in the late 1990s, offering various Jewish thinkers' opinions on the chicken–road issue. It is currently available in this, very old, post from 1998: https://groups.google.com/g/soc.culture.jewish/c/DCON1axavNo?pli=1 (Accessed: 25 July 2024).

6. Leibowitz, Y. (1992) *Judaism, Human Values, and the Jewish State*. Harvard University Press, pp. 31–32.

7. Graham, D. (2024) 'Belonging without believing: British Jewish identity and God', *Institute for Jewish Policy Research*, 20 March. Available at: https://www.jpr.org.uk/insights/belonging-without-believing-british-jewish-identity-and-god (Accessed: 25 July 2024).

8. Cohen, S.M. and Kahn-Harris, K. (2004) *Beyond Belonging: The Jewish Identities of Moderately Engaged British Jews*. London: UJIA / Profile Books.

9. Available at: https://www.youtube.com/ watch?v=Cf4TI9T6Ag8 (Accessed: 25 July 2024).

Chapter Eight: The great Chanukah swindle

1. Also posted at: 'Historic Chanukah lightings show growth of Progressive Judaism' (2023), *The Movement for Reform Judaism*, 15 December. Available at: https://www. reformjudaism.org.uk/historic-chanukah-lightings-show-growth-of-progressive-judaism/ (Accessed: 25 July 2024).

2. Public Menorahs' (no date), *Chabad Lubavitch UK*. Available at: https://www.chabad.org.uk/templates/ articlecco_cdo/aid/828727/jewish/Public-Menorahs.htm (Accessed: 25 July 2024).

3. Jewish Addiction Network (no date): https://www. jaanetwork.org/blog/chanukah-the-festival-of-lights-and-hope (Web page no longer available).

4. Solomon, E. (2022) 'After 90 Years, a Menorah that Symbolized Defiance Is Rekindled in Germany', *The New York Times*, 19 December. Available at: https:// www.nytimes.com/2022/12/19/world/europe/menorah-hanukkah-germany.html (Accessed: 25 July 2024).

5. https://www.watfordfc.com/news/club/news-hornets-and-watford-fc-jewish-supporters-group-celebrate-chanukah (Web page no longer available).

6. Pollard, S. (2024) 'The Speaker's capitulation to the "Free Palestine" mob is a dark day for democracy', *Jewish Chronicle*, 22 February. Available at: https://www. thejc.com/lets-talk/the-speakers-capitulation-to-the-free-palestine-mob-is-a-dark-day-for-democracy-l5kmnb6n (Accessed: 25 July 2024).

7. Kahn-Harris, K. (2016) *Uncivil War: The Israel Conflict in the Jewish Community*. London: David Paul Books.

8. European Commission, Directorate-General for Justice and Consumers (2021) *EU Strategy on Combating Antisemitism and Fostering Jewish Life (2021–2030)*. Available at: https://eur-lex.europa.eu/legal-content/EN/TXT/HTML/?uri=CELEX:52021DC0615. (Accessed: 25 July 2024).

9. Kahn-Harris, K. (2022) 'What we don't know about IHRA: Practices of subversion and neglect', *conflict & communication online*, 21(1). Available at: https://regener-online.de/journalcco/index.htm (Accessed: 1 April 2022).

10. Czollek, M. (2023) *De-Integrate!: A Jewish Survival Guide for the 21st Century*. Translated by J. Cho-Polizzi. Brooklyn: Restless Books.

11. Much of the information in this section is in the public domain via the decision in July 2024 by the Landgericht Frankfurt am Main ruling in favour of Jonathan Schorsh in a law suit bought by Homolka against him.

12. Moser, L. (2023) 'The Rise and Fall of Germany's Most Powerful Rabbi', *Air Mail*. Available at: https://airmail.news/issues/2023-5-6/in-bad-faith (Accessed: 24 April 2024).

13. Ibid.

Chapter Nine: The Israel chapter

1. This is my own translation of one of the two adverts featured in this Hebrew-language video: https://www.youtube.com/watch?v=0DWPLgbCynA (Accessed: 25 July 2024).

2. Blau, U. and Feldman, Y. (2009) 'Gaza Bonanza', *Haaretz (English Edition)*, 11 June. Available at: https://www.haaretz.com/2009-06-11/ty-article/

gaza-bonanza/0000017f-f886-d460-afff-fbe6cf930000 (Accessed: 25 July 2024).

3. Billig, M. (1995) *Banal Nationalism*. SAGE.
4. The text of the poem can be found on many different websites in a number of translations. The particular version that I am not quoting due to copyright clearance issues is: Amichai, Y. (2013) *The Selected Poetry of Yehuda Amichai*. University of California Press, p. 137.
5. Yehoshua, A.B. (1980) *In Praise of Normality. Posen Library of Jewish Culture and Civilization*. Available at: https://www.posenlibrary.com/entry/praise-normality (Accessed: 25 July 2024).
6. Anderson, B. (1991) *Imagined Communities*. 2nd edn. London: Verso.
7. 'Iran attack draws dark humor from captive Israeli audience' (2024) *The Times of Israel*, 14 April. Available at: https://www.timesofisrael.com/iran-attack-draws-dark-humor-from-captive-israeli-audience/ (Accessed: 25 July 2024).
8. The advert was for an 'Earth Day Community Meeting and Teach-In' organised at Cheesman Park, Denver, for 21 April 2024. https://www.codepink.org/co421 (Accessed: 25 July 2024).
9. Bernstein, S. and Rodrigues Fowler, Y. (2024) 'Writers, the time to speak out for Palestine is now!', *Verso*, 22 April. Available at: https://www.versobooks.com/en-gb/blogs/news/society-of-authors-the-time-for-solidarity-is-now (Accessed: 25 July 2024).

Chapter Ten: Sacred smallness

1. Foer, F. (2024) 'The Golden Age of American Jews Is Ending', *The Atlantic*, 4 March. Available at: https://

www.theatlantic.com/magazine/archive/2024/04/us-anti-semitism-jewish-american-safety/677469/ (Accessed: 6 May 2024).

2. Slezkine, Y. (no date) *The Jewish Century*. Princeton: Princeton University Press.

3. https://www.jewbelong.com/about/ (Accessed: 25 July 2024).

4. 10 March 2023.

5. Ben-David, D. (2024) 'Over 100,000 people march through London in solidarity against antisemitism', *Jewish Chronicle*, 26 November. Available at: https://www.thejc.com/news/over-100-000-people-march-in-solidarity-to-protest-antisemitism-in-london-rv7afg9x?s=09 (Accessed: 25 July 2024).

6. Baddiel, D. (2021) *Jews Don't Count*. HarperCollins UK.

7. Hazony, D. (ed.) (2024) *Jewish Priorities: Sixty-Five Proposals for the Future of Our People:* New York: Wicked Son.

8. Magid, S. (2023) *The Necessity of Exile: Essays from a Distance*. New York: Ayin Press.

9. 'Liberal Zionists remain committed to the Zionist notion of a Jewish state in principle and practice, but they recognize that they must tell a different story of Zionism to cohere with these new illiberal realities.' P. 34.

10. Sheldon, R. (2016) *Tragic Encounters and Ordinary Ethics: Palestine-Israel in British Universities*. Manchester University Press.

11. Levy, J. and Baginsky, C. (2023) 'A High Holy Day Message', *The Movement for Reform Judaism*, 7 July. Available at: https://www.reformjudaism.org.uk/a-high-holy-day-message/ (Accessed: 25 July 2024).

12. 'About' (no date) *Jewish Voice for Peace*. Available at:
    https://www.jewishvoiceforpeace.org/about/ (Accessed: 25
    July 2024).

13. Some Jews spell 'God' this way to emphasise the holiness
    of the name through avoiding writing it completely.

14. https://www.tzelem.uk/tzelem-s-philosophy-and-values
    (Website no longer accessible as of 25 July 2024).

15. For example: Neumann, J. (2018) *To Heal the World?:
    How the Jewish Left Corrupts Judaism and Endangers
    Israel*. St. Martin's Publishing Group.

16. Klein, N. (2024) 'We need an exodus from Zionism',
    Guardian, 24 April. Available at: https://www.
    theguardian.com/commentisfree/2024/apr/24/zionism-
    seder-protest-new-york-gaza-israel (Accessed: 25 July
    2024).

17. Brooks, M.P. *et al.* (eds) (2010) '"Nobody's Free Until
    Everybody's Free,": Speech Delivered at the Founding
    of the National Women's Political Caucus, Washington,
    D.C., July 10, 1971', in *The Speeches of Fannie
    Lou Hamer: To Tell It Like It Is*. University Press of
    Mississippi, p. 0. Available at: https://doi.org/10.14325/
    mississippi/9781604738223.003.0017.

18. The letter was revealed by conservative publications but
    appears to be genuine: Kornick, L. (2024) 'Columbia
    Law student group reportedly declares no Jew is safe
    until "everyone is safe"', *Fox News*, 5 May. Available at:
    https://www.foxnews.com/media/columbia-law-student-
    group-reportedly-declares-no-jew-safe-until-everyone-safe
    (Accessed: 25 July 2024).

19. Finlay, J. (2024) 'Empty Chairs: History,
    Politics and Theology', *Torat Albion*, 26 April.
    Available at: https://toratalbion.substack.com/p/

empty-chairs-history-politics-and (Accessed: 25 July 2024).

20. Rosenberg, M. (2024) 'My visit to Israel made me see how British Jews have normalised making themselves smaller', *Jewish News*. Available at: https://www.jewishnews.co.uk/special-report-i-felt-safer-in-an-israel-at-war-with-hamas-than-as-a-jew-in-the-uk/ (Accessed: 25 July 2024).

Chapter Eleven: A small-minded people

1. Brook, S. (1990) *The Club: The Jews of Modern Britain*. London: Pan Books, p. 411.
2. Adorno, T.W. (2001) *The Culture Industry*. London: Routledge Classics, p. 188.
3. Heschel, A.J. (2005) *The Sabbath*. Farrar, Straus and Giroux.
4. For example: 'Want to Divest from Israel? Better Get Rid of Your iPhone' (2024), *Newsweek*, 23 May. Available at: https://www.newsweek.com/want-divest-israel-better-get-rid-your-iphone-opinion-1904189 (Accessed: 25 July 2024).
5. Heilman, S.C. (1983) *People of the Book: Drama, Fellowship and Religion*. Chicago: University of Chicago Press.
6. Gidley, B., McGeever, B. and Feldman, D. (2020) 'Labour and Antisemitism: a Crisis Misunderstood', *The Political Quarterly*, 91(2), pp. 413–21. Available at: https://doi.org/10.1111/1467-923X.12854.
7. Jacobson, H. (2024) 'Is this the end of Israel? Six Months on, Jews are starting to lose faith', *UnHerd*, 6 April. Available at: https://unherd.com/2024/04/is-this-the-end-of-israel/ (Accessed: 25 July 2024).

8. Weisel is recorded as writing these words in 1986, but it appears that versions of the quote have been circulating since the nineteenth century.
9. Finkelstein, D. (2023) *Hitler, Stalin, Mum and Dad: A Family Memoir of Miraculous Survival*. HarperCollins UK.
10. Ibid., p. 23.

Conclusion

1. Quoted in: Sutcliffe, A. (2020) *What Are Jews For?: History, Peoplehood, and Purpose*. Princeton University Press, p. 1.
2. Ibid.
3. Ibid., p. 290.
4. Heller, N. (2024) 'The Battle for Attention', 29 April. Available at: https://www.newyorker.com/magazine/2024/05/06/the-battle-for-attention (Accessed: 25 July 2024).